A LENT SOURCEBOOK:
The Forty Days

BOOK TWO
*Tuesday of the Third Week of Lent
to Holy Thursday*

Also in the Sourcebook Series:

A LENT SOURCEBOOK:
The Forty Days

Edited by
J. Robert Baker
Evelyn Kaehler
Peter Mazar

Art by
Suzanne M. Novak

LTP Liturgy Training Publications

Acknowledgments

The texts in this book were gathered by J. Robert Baker, James P. Barron, OP (who chose and translated several Polish texts for this book), Thomas Cademartrie, Elizabeth Hoffman, Gabe Huck, Evelyn Kaehler, Peter Mazar, Mary McGann, RSCJ, G. Michael Thompson (who chose and translated many of the texts from the Byzantine tradition for this book) and Elizabeth-Anne Vanek. Our heartfelt thanks to all these folks!

We are grateful to the many publishers and authors who have given permission to include their work. Every effort has been made to determine the ownership of all texts and to make proper arrangements for their use. Any oversight that may have occurred, if brought to our attention, will gladly be corrected in future editions.

Acknowledgments for sources not listed below will be found in the endnotes.

Scripture texts used in this work, unless otherwise noted, are adapted from *The New Revised Standard Version Bible,* © 1989, Division of Christian Education of the National Council of the Churches of Christ in the United States of America. Published by Oxford University Press, Inc., 200 Madison Avenue, New York NY 10016. Used with permission.

Excerpts from the English translation of *Rite of Marriage* © 1969, International Committee on English in the Liturgy, Inc. (ICEL); excerpts from the English translation of *The Roman Missal* © 1973, ICEL; excerpts from the English translation of *The Liturgy of the Hours* © 1974, ICEL; excerpts from the English translation of *Rite of Penance* © 1974, ICEL; text of "Our Father, We Have Wandered" from the *Resource Collection of Hymns and Service Music for the Liturgy* © 1981, ICEL; excerpts from the English translation of *Rite of Christian Initiation of Adults* © 1985, ICEL; excerpts from the English translation of *Collection of Masses of the Blessed Virgin Mary* © 1987, 1989, ICEL; excerpts from the English translation of *Book of Blessings* © 1988, ICEL; excerpts from the English translation of *Ceremonial of Bishops* © 1989, ICEL. All rights reserved.

Copy editor/Permissions editor: Theresa Pincich
Editorial assistance: Lorraine Schmidt
Production: Jill Smith and Phyllis Martinez
Series designer: Michael Tapia

Contents

An Order
for
Daily Prayer

Hymn

These songs may be sung to any long-meter tune, such as "Praise God from whom all blessings flow," or "The glory of these forty days." Or substitute one of the other hymns found throughout this book.

For morning:

Again we keep this solemn fast,
A gift of faith from ages past,
This Lent which binds us lovingly
To faith and hope and charity.

More sparing, therefore, let us make
The words we speak, the food we take,
Our sleep, our laughter, ev'ry sense;
Learn peace through holy penitence.

For evening:

O Sun of justice, Jesus Christ,
Dispel the darkness of our hearts,
Till your blest light makes nighttime flee
And brings the joys your day imparts.

Behold the happy day shall dawn
When in your light earth blooms anew;
Led back again to life's true way,
May we, forgiv'n, rejoice in you.

Psalm

Option 1, Psalm 137

By the rivers of Babylon—
there we sat down and there we wept
    when we remembered Zion.
On the willows there
    we hung up our harps.
For there our captors
    asked us for songs,
and our tormentors asked for mirth, saying,
    "Sing us one of the songs of Zion!"
How could we sing the LORD's song
    in a foreign land?
If I forget you, O Jerusalem,
    let my right hand wither!
Let my tongue cling to the roof of my mouth,
    if I do not remember you,
if I do not set Jerusalem
    above my highest joy.

Option 2, Psalm 51

Have mercy on me, O God,
according to your steadfast love;
according to your abundant mercy
   blot out my transgressions.
Wash me thoroughly from my iniquity,
   and cleanse me from my sin.
For I know my transgressions,
   and my sin is ever before me.
Against you, you alone, have I sinned,
   and done what is evil in your sight,
so that you are justified in your sentence
   and blameless when you pass judgment.
Indeed, I was born guilty,
   a sinner when my mother conceived me.

You desire truth in the inward being;
   therefore teach me wisdom in my secret heart.
Purge me with hyssop, and I shall be clean;
   wash me, and I shall be whiter than snow.
Let me hear joy and gladness;
   let the bones that you have crushed rejoice.
Hide your face from my sins,
   and blot out all my iniquities.
Create in me a clean heart, O God,
   and put a new and right spirit within me.
Do not cast me away from your presence,
   and do not take your holy spirit from me.
Restore to me the joy of your salvation,
   and sustain in me a willing spirit.

Option 3, Psalm 91

You live in God's secret place;
The Most High shades your sleep.
You say to the Lord, "My strong refuge,
   My God, in whom I trust."
God saves you from fowlers' snares,
   And from deadly disease.
The Lord's pinions are over you;
   You hide beneath God's wings.
Do not fear the terror of night,
   Or the arrow that flies by day,
The pestilence stalking in darkness,
   The plague laying waste at noon.
A thousand may fall at your side,
   Ten thousand at your right hand;
But you will not be stricken—
   The faithful God is your shield and tower.
Only look with your eyes,
   And see the oppressors punished.
As for you, the Lord is your refuge;
   You have made the Most High your shelter.
Evil will not befall you,
   Nor harm approach your tent.
On your behalf, God commanded the angels
   To guard you in all your ways.
Their hands will lift you high,
   Lest you catch your foot on a stone.
You shall step on lion and snake,
   Tread down young lion and serpent.
"I will save those who cling to me,
   And protect those who know my name.
They call and I answer them;
   I am with them in their distress.
I will rescue them and reward them;
   I satisfy them with long life,
      And show them my saving power."

Option 4, Psalm 130

Out of the depths I cry to you, O LORD.
   LORD, hear my voice!
Let your ears be attentive
   to the voice of my supplications!

If you, O LORD, should mark iniquities,
   LORD, who could stand?
But there is forgiveness with you,
   so that you may be revered.

I wait for you, LORD, my soul waits,
   and in your word I hope;
my soul waits for you
   more than those who watch for the morning,
   more than those who watch for the morning.

O Israel, hope in the LORD!
   For with you, LORD, there is steadfast love,
   and with you is great power to redeem.
You will redeem Israel
   from all its iniquities.

Option 5

The psalms and the passages from the psalms found within the proper day may be prayed at this time.

Verse of the day

Read the short scripture verse at the head of the proper day.

Meditation

Read one or more of the texts for the proper day.

Silence

Gospel Canticle

For morning:
Blessed are you, O Lord, the God of Israel!
You have come to your people and set them free.
You have raised up for us a horn of deliverance
    in the house of your servant David.
Through the mouth of your holy prophets of old
you promised liberation from our enemies,
from the hands of all who hate us.

You promised to show mercy to our forebears
and to remember your holy covenant.
This was the oath you swore to our father Abraham:
that, rescued from the hands of our enemies,
we are free to worship you without fear,
holy and righteous in your sight
all the days of our life.

You, my child, shall be called the prophet of the Most High,
for you will go before the Lord to prepare the way,
to give God's people knowledge of salvation
    by the forgiveness of their sins.
In the tender compassion of our God
the morning sun will break upon us,
to shine on those who dwell in darkness
    and the shadow of death,
and to guide our feet in the way of peace.

Luke 1:68–79

For evening:

My soul magnifies the Lord,
and my spirit rejoices in God my Savior
who has looked with favor on me, a lowly serving maid.
From this day all generations will call me blessed.

The Mighty One has done great things for me:
holy the name of the Lord,
whose mercy is on the God-fearing
from generation to generation.
The arm of the Lord is filled with strength,
scattering the proudhearted.
God cast the mighty from their thrones,
lifting up the lowly.
God filled the hungry with good things,
sending the rich away empty.

God has come to the help of Israel, the Lord's servant,
remembering mercy,
the mercy promised to our forebears,
to Abraham and his children for ever.

Luke 1:46–55

Intercessions and Lord's Prayer

Pray in Jesus' name for the world, the church, the poor and oppressed, the sick and the dying, our neighbors and friends, our families and ourselves. At the end, all the prayers are sealed with the Lord's Prayer.

 ## Almsgiving

This might be the moment, as prayer concludes, to add money to an almsbox. Of course, all our daily works of prayer, fasting and the giving of charity will make of our Lent one continual prayer, one unending act of praise.

K EEP me as the apple of your eye;
hide me in the shadow of your wings.

Psalm 17:8

I sing as I arise today!
I call on my Creator's might:
The will of God to be my guide,
The eye of God to be my sight,
The word of God to be my speech,
The hand of God to be my stay,
The shield of God to be my strength,
The path of God to be my way.

Patrick of Ireland
Fifth century

THE presidents and satraps conspired and came to the king and said to him, "O King Darius, live forever! All the presidents of the kingdom, the prefects and the satraps, the counselors and the governors are agreed that the king should establish an ordinance and enforce an interdict, that whoever prays to anyone, divine or human, for thirty days, except to you, O king, shall be thrown into a den of lions. Now, O king, establish the interdict and sign the document, so that it cannot be changed, according to the law of the Medes and the Persians, which cannot be revoked." Therefore King Darius signed the document and interdict.

Although Daniel knew that the document had been signed, he continued to go to his house, which had windows in its upper room open toward Jerusalem, and to get down on his knees three times a day to pray to his God and praise God, just as he had done previously. The conspirators came and found Daniel praying and seeking mercy before his God. Then they approached the king and said concerning the interdict, "O king! Did you not sign an interdict, that anyone who prays to anyone, divine or human, within thirty days except to you, O king, shall be thrown into a den of lions?" The king answered, "The thing stands fast, according to the law of the Medes and Persians, which cannot be revoked." Then they responded to the king, "Daniel, one of the exiles from Judah, pays no attention to you, O king, or to the interdict you have signed, but he is saying his prayers three times a day."

When the king heard the charge, he was very much distressed. He was determined to save Daniel, and until the sun went down he made every effort to rescue him. Then the conspirators came to the king and said to him, "Know, O king, that it is a law of the Medes and Persians that no interdict or ordinance that the king establishes can be changed."

Then the king gave the command, and Daniel was brought and thrown into the den of lions. The king said to Daniel, "May your God, whom you faithfully serve, deliver you!" A stone was brought and laid on the mouth of the den, and the king sealed it with his own signet and with the signet of his lords, so that nothing might be changed concerning Daniel. Then the king went to his palace and spent the night fasting;

Daniel 6:6–18   no food was brought to him, and sleep fled from him.

TRULY the eye of the LORD is on those who fear God,
  on those who hope in God's steadfast love,
to deliver their soul from death,
Psalm 33:18–19   and to keep them alive in famine.

ALL right, Mr. Death. See now. . . . I'm gonna tell you what I'm gonna do. I'm gonna take and build me a fence around this yard. See? I'm gonna build me a fence around what belongs to me. And then I want you to stay on the other side. See? You stay over there until you're ready for me. Then you come on. Bring your army. Bring your sickle. Bring your wrestling clothes. I ain't gonna fall down on my vigilance this time. You ain't gonna sneak up on me no more. When you ready for me, when the top of your list say Troy Maxson, that's when you come around here. You come up and knock on the front door and ask for me. Then we gonna find out what manner of man you are. Ain't nobody else got nothing to do

with this. This is between you and me. Man to man. You stay
on the other side of that fence until you ready for me. Then
you come up and knock on the front door. Anytime you want.
I'll be ready for you.

August Wilson

K YRIE, O God the Holy Ghost,
Guard our faith, the gift we need the most,
And bless our life's last hour,
That we leave this sinful world with gladness.
    Eleison, eleison!

Latin hymn
Eleventh century

L ORD, I keep so busy praising my Jesus,
Keep so busy praising my Jesus,
Keep so busy praising my Jesus,
Ain't got time to die.
'Cause when I'm healing the sick,
I'm praising my Jesus.
Yes, I'm praising my Jesus when I'm healing the sick.
Lord, I ain't got time to die.

Lord, I keep so busy working for the kingdom,
Keep so busy working for the kingdom,
Keep so busy working for the kingdom,
Ain't got time to die.
'Cause when I'm feeding the poor,
I'm working for the kingdom.
Yes, I'm working when I'm feeding the poor.
Lord, I ain't got time to die.

    'Cause it takes all of my time to praise my Jesus,
    All of my time to praise my Lord.
    If I don't praise him, the rocks gonna cry out,
    "Glory and honor, glory and honor!"
    Ain't got time to die.

Hall Johnson

HEAR a just cause, O LORD; attend to my cry;
give ear to my prayer from lips free of deceit.
From you let my vindication come;
  let your eyes see the right.

If you try my heart, if you visit me by night,
  if you test me, you will find no wickedness in me;
  my mouth does not transgress.
As for what others do, by the word of your lips
  I have avoided the ways of the violent.
My steps have held fast to your paths;
  my feet have not slipped.

I call upon you, for you will answer me, O God;
  incline your ear to me, hear my words.
Wondrously show your steadfast love,
  O savior of those who seek refuge
  from their adversaries at your right hand.

Guard me as the apple of the eye;
  hide me in the shadow of your wings,
from the wicked who despoil me,
  my deadly enemies who surround me.
They close their hearts to pity;
  with their mouths they speak arrogantly.
They track me down; now they surround me;
  they set their eyes to cast me to the ground.
They are like a lion eager to tear,
  like a young lion lurking in ambush.

Rise up, O LORD, confront them, overthrow them!
  By your sword deliver my life from the wicked,
from mortals—by your hand, O LORD—

Psalm 17:1–14   from mortals whose portion in life is in this world.

N O longer does prayer bring an angel of dew to the heart of a fiery furnace, or close up the mouths of lions, or transport to the hungry food from the fields. No longer does it remove all sense of pain by the grace it wins for others. But it gives the armor of patience to those who suffer, who feel pain, who are distressed. It strengthens the power of grace, so that faith may know what it is gaining from the Lord and understand what it is suffering for the name of God.

Tertullian
Third century

Y OU will tread on the lion and the adder,
the young lion and the serpent
you will trample under foot.

Psalm 91:13

T HUS it was that when Daniel was shut in the lion-pit by the king's orders, God sent him his dinner, and the hungry beasts left the man of God alone and let him take his food. So too, Elias was fed on his flight, in his seclusion and in time of persecution; he was served by ravens, his food brought by birds. Yes, wild beasts can keep their distance, birds can wait at table, but the human will is so horribly cruel that people are always on the prowl, always ready to pounce on their prey.

Cyprian of Carthage
Third century

L ET the mouth also fast from disgraceful speeches and railings. For what does it profit if we abstain from fish and fowl and yet bite and devour our brothers and sisters? The evil speaker eats the flesh of his brother and bites the body of his neighbor.

John Chrysostom
Fourth century

Bertold Brecht

WHAT keeps a person alive?
  To live on others.
To enjoy nibbling them first,
  then eating them whole.
To forget that they were ever
  one's own brothers and sisters.

REAL leadership begins not with a "hard-nosed plan" or a "can-do attitude," but with what the ancient Chinese philosopher Chuang Tzu called *"the fasting of the heart."* The phrase appears in one of Chuang Tzu's stories, which describes a discussion between the great teacher Confucius and his eager young student Yen Hui. Yen Hui had come to Confucius with a plan to reform the government of a Chinese province whose leader was overwhelmingly self-serving and blind to his people's needs. In a torrent of well-intentioned verbiage, Yen Hui explains to Confucius how he will reform the province through a program of enlightened, blameless leadership. Confucius, instead of approving the youngster's enthusiasm, tells Yen Hui he must learn to let go of all his plans—*to fast in the heart*—before he can find the wisdom needed to be of service to the people.

"Fasting of the heart frees you from limitation and from preoccupation. Fasting of the heart begets unity and freedom. . . . Look at this window: it is nothing but a hole in the wall, but because of it the whole room is full of light. So when the faculties are empty, the heart is full of light. Being full of light, it becomes an influence by which others are secretly transformed."

This letting go, this fasting of the heart, is perhaps what Jesus had in mind when he said, "The eye is the lamp of the body."

Nathan Mitchell

S O, if your eye is healthy, your whole body will be full of light; but if your eye is unhealthy, your whole body will be full of darkness. If then the light in you is darkness, how great is the darkness! Matthew 6:22–23

Y OU may not enter the heavenly Jerusalem by contempla- tion unless you go in through the blood of the Lamb as through a door. Nor are you prepared in any way for divine contemplation that leads to the ecstasies of the mind unless you are, like Daniel, a man of desires. Such desires are aroused in us in two different ways: the first is through the outcry of prayer, which makes us roar with anguish of heart; the second, through the flash of intuition, by which the mind turns itself most directly and intently toward the light.

Therefore, I invite the reader to cry out in prayer through Christ crucified, by whose blood we are cleansed from the filth of sin. Let us not believe that it is enough to read with- out unction, to speculate without devotion, to investigate without godly zeal, to know without love, to understand without humility, to strive without divine grace, or to reflect as a mirror without divinely inspired wisdom.

Bonaventure
Thirteenth century

D ISCIPLINE yourselves, keep alert. Like a roaring lion your adversary the devil prowls around, looking for some- one to devour. Resist him, steadfast in your faith, for you know that your brothers and sisters in all the world are undergoing the same kinds of suffering. And after you have suffered for a little while, the God of all grace, who has called you to eternal glory in Christ, will restore, support, strengthen, and establish you. 1 Peter 5:8–10

D E ore leonis libera me, Domine.
Et a cornibus unicornium humilitatem meam.

From the lion's mouth deliver me, Lord.

Monastic liturgy From the horns of unicorns deliver my miserable life.

S AMSON went down with his father and mother to Timnah. When he came to the vineyards of Timnah, suddenly a young lion roared at him. The spirit of the LORD rushed on him, and he tore the lion apart barehanded as one might tear apart a kid. But he did not tell his father or his mother what he had done. After a while he returned and he turned aside to see the carcass of the lion, and there was a swarm of bees in the body of the lion, and honey. He scraped it out into his hands, and went on, eating as he went. When he came to his father and mother, he gave some to them, and they ate it. But he did not tell them that he had taken the honey from the carcass of the lion.

Samson said "Let me now put a riddle to you." So they said to him, "Ask your riddle; let us hear it." He said to them,

"Out of the eater came something to eat.
Out of the strong came something sweet."

Judges 14:5–6, 8–9, 12, 13–14 But they could not explain the riddle.

T HUS the lion yields me honey;
From the eater food is given;
Strengthen'd thus, I still press forward,
Singing as I wade to heaven:
    Sweet affliction, sweet affliction,
    And my sins are all forgiven!
    Sweet affliction, sweet affliction,
Early American hymn   And my sins are all forgiven!

TAKE to heart these words which I enjoin on you today. Drill them into your children. Speak of them at home and abroad, whether you are busy or at rest.

Deuteronomy 6:6–7

NOW this is the commandment—the statutes and the ordinances—that the LORD your God charged me to teach you to observe in the land that you are about to cross into and occupy, so that you and your children and your children's children may fear the LORD your God all the days of your life, and keep all the decrees and the commandments that I am commanding you, so that your days may be long. Hear therefore, O Israel, and observe them diligently, so that it may go well with you and so that you may multiply greatly in a land flowing with milk and honey, as the LORD, the God of your ancestors, has promised you.

Hear, O Israel: The LORD is our God, the LORD alone. You shall love the LORD your God with all your heart, and with all your soul, and with all your might.

Deuteronomy 6:1–5

DO not think that I have come to abolish the law or the prophets; I have come not to abolish but to fulfill. For truly I tell you, until heaven and earth pass away, not one letter, not one stroke of a letter, will pass from the law until all is accomplished. Therefore, whoever breaks one of the least of these commandments, and teaches others to do the same, will be called least in the kingdom of heaven; but whoever does them and teaches them will be called great in the kingdom of heaven.

Matthew 5:17–19

W E do not know in any great detail about the salvation of the whole universe. We do not know, simply because God has not chosen to tell us very much. But this much we do know: The world as we now know it will die and be destroyed, just as we die and our terrestrial existence as we now know it will go down in death and decay. But just as the body will rise and be transformed in Christ, transfigured in Christ, so will the created universe rise in Christ and be transformed in Christ, transfigured in Christ.

Kilian McDonnell

T HE liturgy is cosmic art. The reality revealed is the answer to the age-old dreams of the universe, of that creation which is in travail even till now; and again it is both a response and an offering and a cleansing, for this returning of the universe to the Life is itself a renewal of life, a healing and sanctifying and blessing. So, if you learn through the church's liturgy to be clean of heart, you do three things: You achieve a personal integrity through a worship which is neither rational nor emotional but total, and therefore a total renewal of the self; you recover something of the integrity of the self in the cosmic family and share in some degree in the bringing back of the cosmos to its source; you respond to that divine power which will give you the essential integrity without which nothing else is of importance: the integrity of the self in the infinity of God.

Gerald Vann

O NE may understand the cosmos, but never the ego; the self is more distant than any star. Thou shalt love the Lord thy God; but thou shalt not know thyself. We are all under the same mental calamity; we have all forgotten our names. We have all forgotten what we really are. All that we call common sense and rationality and practicality and positivism only means that for certain dead levels of our life we forget that we have forgotten. All that we call spirit and art and ecstasy only means that for one awful instant we remember that we forget.

G. K. Chesterton

WE have to remember that we can't remember. My fear really is that memory itself is in exile. The only possible salvation of the Jewish people is to remember our whole experience. But this memory is so powerful, so exalted, that we can't remember fully: It is bigger than us, bigger than all of us, than all the people. So how do you transform it into memory? Memory must not stop. If I were to stop in, let's say, 1944, it would lead to madness. And then I realize that, after all, there was a Jewish life before, and there I find my friends and my teachers, and I go back and find my grandparents, and go back and I find the Hasidim, and go back and find the Kabbalists, and I go back—memory must go back until it goes back to the source of memory.

Elie Wiesel

TAKE care and watch yourselves closely, so as neither to forget the things that your eyes have seen nor to let them slip from your mind all the days of your life; make them known to your children and your children's children—how you once stood before the LORD at Horeb.

Deuteronomy 4:9–10

MY dear children, perhaps you will not understand what I'm going to say to you now, for I often speak very incomprehensibly, but, I'm sure, you will remember that there's nothing higher, stronger, more wholesome and more useful in life than some good memory, especially when it goes back to the days of your childhood, to the days of your life at home. You are told a lot about your education, but some beautiful, sacred memory, preserved since childhood, is perhaps the best education of all. If a man carries many such memories into life with him, he is saved for the rest of his days. And even if only one good memory is left in our hearts, it may also be the instrument of our salvation one day.

Fyodor Dostoyevsky
Nineteenth century

Alexander Schmemann

W HAT must be stopped during Lent is the "addiction" to TV—the transformation of a person into a vegetable in an armchair, glued to the screen and passively accepting anything coming from it. When I was a child (this was the pre-TV era) my mother used to lock the piano during the first, fourth and seventh weeks of Lent. I remember this more vividly than the long lenten services, and even today a radio playing during Lent shocks me as almost a blasphemy. This personal recollection is only an illustration of the impact some very external decisions can have on a child's soul. And what is involved here is not a mere isolated custom or rule but the experience of Lent as a special time, as something which is constantly present and must not be lost, mutilated or destroyed.

I prefer to cut children's spiritual garments a little large, for them to grow into, as they will in time. And who knows what vivid image or hint of the beauty of God may remain in their mind and memory?

Dorothy Coddington

I sometimes fear the younger generation will be deprived of the pleasures of hoeing;
  there is no knowing
how many souls have been formed by this simple exercise.

The dry earth like a great scab breaks, revealing
    moist-dark loam—
    the pea-root's home,
a fertile wound perpetually healing.

How neatly the green weeds go under!
    The blade chops the earth new.
    Ignorant the wise boy who
has never performed this simple, stupid and useful wonder.

John Updike

PEOPLE were bringing even infants to Jesus that he might touch them; and when the disciples saw it, they sternly ordered them not to do it. But Jesus called for them and said, "Let the little children come to me, and do not stop them; for it is to such as these that the kingdom of God belongs. Truly I tell you, whoever does not receive the kingdom of God as a little child will never enter it.   Luke 18:15–17

BABIES and small children are pure beauty, love, joy—the truest in this world. But the thorns are there of night watches, of illnesses, of infant perversities and contrariness. There are glimpses of heaven and hell.   Dorothy Day

OUT of the mouths of babes and infants
    you have founded a bulwark because of your foes,
    to silence the enemy and the avenger.

When I look at your heavens, the work of your fingers,
    the moon and the stars that you have established;
what are human beings that you are mindful of them,
    mortals that you care for them?

Yet you have made them a little lower than God,
    and crowned them with glory and honor.   Psalm 8:2–5

LIKE a little drop of water in a quantity of wine, or red-hot iron in the burning flame, we take on the character of that in which we are immersed. But this deification, which is our ultimate destiny, can never be complete and permanent in this life. Nor indeed even in the next can our loss to ourselves be complete, until God's total intentions for us are fulfilled in the resurrection of our bodies.   Aelred Squire

WHEN from the dust of death I rise
To claim my mansion in the skies,
This then shall be my only plea:
Christ Jesus lived and died for me.

Nicolaus L.
von Zinzendorf
Eighteenth century

WHO gave you the power to behold the beauty of the heavens, the sun in its course, the moon, the myriads of stars with the harmony and order that are theirs like the music of a lyre? Who has blessed you with rain, crops to cultivate, food, arts and crafts, homes, laws, organized society, civilized life with friendship and family ties? Who gave you animals to tame for your service and others to be your food? Who has made you lord and master of everything on earth? In short, who was the giver of all the gifts that make human beings superior to other creatures?

Was it not God, whose first request to us now is that we should show generosity in return? Having already received so much from God and hoping for so much more, we should surely be ashamed to refuse God the one thing asked of us, which is to show generosity to others. When our Lord and God is not ashamed to be called our Father, can we repudiate our own kith and kin?

Gregory of Nazianzus
Fourth century

REMEMBER the long way that the LORD your God has led you these forty years in the wilderness, in order to humble you, testing you to know what was in your heart, whether or not you would keep the commandments. God humbled you by letting you hunger, then by feeding you with manna, with which neither you nor your ancestors were acquainted, in order to make you understand that one does not live by bread alone, but by every word that comes from the mouth of the LORD. The clothes on your back did not wear out and your feet did not swell these forty years. Know then in your heart that as a parent disciplines a child, so the LORD your God disciplines you. Therefore keep the commandments of the LORD your God, by walking in God's ways and by fearing the LORD.

Deuteronomy 8:2–6

N OW that faith has come, we are no longer subject to a disciplinarian, for in Christ Jesus you are all children of God through faith. As many of you as were baptized into Christ have clothed yourselves with Christ.

Galatians 3:25–27

H OW beautiful are those, and how blessed they be, Who in deep tribulation daily follow me.
I have a robe divinely fair for such children to wear,
And a crown shining bright they shall wear with delight,
When done with the fading things of time.

Shaker hymn

S ISTER, may you grow into thousands of myriads.

Genesis 24:60

D EAR Lord, we are now in the holy season of Lent. We begin to realize anew that these are the days of salvation, these are the acceptable days. We know that we are all sinners. We know that sin destroys your life in us as a drought withers the leaves and chokes the life from the land, leaving an arid, dusty desert. Every day we are so often reminded in field and wood, in sky and stream, of your own boundless generosity to us. Help us to realize that you are never outdone in generosity, and that the least thing we do for you will be rewarded, full measure, pressed down, shaken together, and flowing over. Then we shall see how the desert can blossom, and the dry and wasted land can bring forth the rich, useful fruit that was expected of it from the beginning.

*The Rural Life
Prayerbook*

THE wilderness and the dry land shall be glad,
the desert shall rejoice and blossom;
like the crocus it shall blossom abundantly,
and rejoice with joy and singing.
For waters shall break forth in the wilderness,
and streams in the desert;
the burning sand shall become a pond,
and the thirsty ground springs of water.

Isaiah 35:1–2, 6–7

O healing river, send down your waters,
Send down your waters upon this land.
O healing river, send down your waters,
And wash the blood from off the sand.

This land is parching; this land is burning;
No seed is growing in the barren ground.
O healing river, send down your waters;
O healing river, send your waters down.

Let the seed of freedom awake and flourish;
Let the deep roots nourish; let the tall stalks rise.
O healing river, send down your waters,
O healing river, from out of the skies.

Baptist hymn

IT was toward evening, the time when women go out to draw water. And Isaac said, "O LORD, God of my master Abraham, please grant me success today and show steadfast love to my master Abraham. I am standing here by the spring of water, and the daughters of the townspeople are coming out to draw water. Let the girl to whom I shall say, 'Please offer your jar that I may drink,' and who shall say, 'Drink, and I will water your camels'—let her be the one whom you have appointed for your servant Isaac. By this I shall know that you have shown steadfast love to my master."

Before he had finished speaking, there was Rebekah, who was born to Bethuel son of Milcah, the wife of Nabor, Abraham's brother, coming out with her water jar on her shoulder. The girl was very fair to look upon, a virgin, whom no man had known.

Genesis 24:11–16

A spendthrift lover is the Lord
Who never counts the cost
Or asks if heaven can afford
To woo a world that's lost.
Our lover tosses coins of gold
Across the midnight skies
And stokes the sun against the cold
To warm us when we rise.

Still more is spent in blood and tears
To win the human heart,
To overcome the violent fears
That drive the world apart.
Behold the bruised and thorn-crowned face
Of one who bears our scars
And empties out the wealth of grace
That's hinted by the stars.

How shall we love this heart-strong God
Who gives us ev'rything,
Whose ways to us are strange and odd,
What can we give or bring?
Acceptance of the matchless gift
Is gift enough to give.
The very act will shake and shift
The way we love and live.

Thomas H. Troeger

A garden locked is my sister, my bride,
a garden locked, a fountain sealed.
A garden fountain, a well of living water,
and flowing streams of Lebanon.

Song of Songs 4:12, 15

REBEKAH went down to the spring, filled her jar, and came up. Then the servant ran to meet her and said, "Please let me sip a little water from your jar." "Drink, my lord," she said, and quickly lowered her jar upon her hand and gave him a drink. When she had finished giving him a drink, she said, "I will draw for your camels also, until they have finished drinking." So she quickly emptied her jar into the trough and ran again to the well to draw, and she drew for all his camels. The man gazed at her in silence.

Genesis 24:16–21

ENTER into the mystery of silence.

Your goal in life is not to hold your tongue but to love, to know yourself and to receive your God. You need to learn how to listen, how to retreat into the depths, how to rise above yourself.

Silence leads you to all this, so seek it lovingly and vigilantly. But beware of false silence: Yours should be neither taciturnity nor glumness, nor should it be systematic or inflexible, or torpid. Authentic silence is the gateway to peace, adoration and love.

Live your silence, don't merely endure it.

Pierre-Marie Delfieux

WHEN words are many, transgression is not lacking, but the prudent are restrained in speech.

Proverbs 10:19

MEN of few words are the best men.

William Shakespeare
Sixteenth century

SILENCE goes hand in hand with fasting.

Jean-Paul Aron

EVERY year Benedict met with his sister, Scholastica, to spend the whole day in the praise of God and in holy conversation. At their last meeting it turned out that, because of his sister's love and the power of her prayer, they spent the whole night in vigil and comforted each other with holy converse in spiritual things. But he did this seldom—once a year. This once was so meaningful, so gratifying, because it was filled with and permeated by a year's silence. It was like a seed's bursting forth after long months of quietly maturing, to grow, to blossom and to bear fruit.

Emmanuel Heufelder

YOU know that good makes no noise and noise does no good. In the common life calm is necessary for the brothers and sisters who are praying, reading and writing, or at night, resting. For love, then, watch your step, your work, your greetings and your speech. Silence too is charity.

Pierre Marie Delfieux

DEATH and life are in the power of the tongue, and those who love it will eat its fruits.

Proverbs 18:21

John of the Cross
Sixteenth century

THE language that God hears best is the silent language of love.

I am as rich as God.
Each dust mote
more or less
do I in common
with my God possess.

See what no eye can see,
go where no foot can go,
choose that which is no choice—
then you may hear

Angelus Silesius
Seventeenth century

what makes no sound—
God's voice.

Genesis 24:63–67

ISAAC went out in the evening to walk in the field; and looking up, he saw camels coming. And Rebekah looked up, and when she saw Isaac, she slipped quickly from the camel and said to the servant, "Who is the man over there, walking in the field to meet us?" The servant said, "It is my master." So she took her veil and covered herself. And the servant told Isaac all the things that he had done. Then Isaac brought her into his mother Sarah's tent. He took Rebekah, and she became his wife; and he loved her. So Isaac was comforted after his mother's death.

M AY the peace of Christ live always in your hearts
and in your home.
May you have true friends to stand by you,
    both in joy and in sorrow.
May you be ready and willing to help and comfort
    all who come to you in need.
And may the blessings promised to the compassionate
    be yours in abundance.

May you find happiness and satisfaction in your work.
May daily problems never cause you undue anxiety,
        nor the desire for earthly possessions
        dominate your lives.
But may your hearts' first desire be always the good things
    waiting for you in the life of heaven.   *Rite of Marriage*

J ERUSALEM, glorify the Lord;
Zion, praise your God,
Who strengthens the bars of your gates;
    And blesses the children within you;
Who makes your country prosperous,
    And satisfies you with plump grain;
Whose command directs the world,
    Whose word runs so swiftly;
Who sends the snow, heaped up like wool,
    Who scatters the frost like dust,
Who hurls down icy bits of hail—
    Can anyone stand before God's bitter cold?
But God speaks again, and all of it melts;
    God turns the wind, and the waters flow.   Psalm 147:12–18

THIS is the frost coming out of the ground;
  this is spring.
It precedes the green and flowery spring,
as mythology precedes regular poetry. . . .
It convinces me that earth is still in her swaddling-clothes,
and stretches forth baby fingers on every side.

Henry David Thoreau
Nineteenth century

LENTEN ys come with love to toune,
  With blosmen and with briddes roune,
    That al this blisse bryngeth;
Dayes-eyes in this dales,
Notes suete of nyhtegales,
    Uch foul song singeth;

The threstelcoc him threteth oo,
Away is huere wynter wo,
    When woderove springeth;
Thise foules singeth ferly fele,
Ant wlyteth on huere wunne wele,
    That al the wode ryngeth.

Anonymous
Thirteenth century

WE must remember the original meaning of Lent, as the
  ver sacrum, the church's "holy spring" in which the
catechumens were prepared for their baptism, and public
penitents were made ready by penance for their restoration to
the sacramental life in a communion with the rest of the
church. Lent is then not a season of punishment so much as
one of healing.

Thomas Merton

A N altered look about the hills;
A Tyrian light the village fills;
A wider sunrise in the dawn;
A deeper twilight on the lawn;
A print of a vermillion foot;
A purple finger on the slope;
A flippant fly upon the pane;
A spider at his trade again;
An added strut in chanticleer;
A flower expected everywhere;
An axe shrill singing in the woods;
Fern-odors on untravelled roads,
All this, and more I cannot tell,
A furtive look you know as well,
And Nicodemus' mystery

Emily Dickinson

Receives its annual reply.

Nineteenth century

T HERE was a Pharisee named Nicodemus, a leader of the Jews. He came to Jesus by night and said to him, "Rabbi, we know that you are a teacher who has come from God; for no one can do these signs that you do apart from the presence of God." Jesus answered him, "Very truly, I tell you, no one can see the kingdom of God without being born from above." Nicodemus said to him, "How can anyone be born after having grown old? Can one enter a second time into the mother's womb and be born?" Jesus answered, "Very truly, I tell you, no one can enter the kingdom of God without being born of water and Spirit. What is born of the flesh is flesh, and what is born of the Spirit is spirit. Do not be astonished that I said to you, 'You must be born from above.' The wind blows where it chooses, and you hear the sound of it, but you do not know where it comes from or where it goes. So it is with everyone who is born of the Spirit."

John 3:1–8

A WAKE, O north wind,
and come, O south wind!
Blow upon my garden
Song of Songs 4:16   that its fragrance may be wafted abroad.

G OD of our forebears and God of all creation,
we ask you to look favorably on your servants;
make them fervent in spirit,
joyful in hope,
and always ready to serve your name.

Lead them, Lord, to the baptism of new birth,
Rite of Christian   so that, living a fruitful life in the company of your faithful,
Initiation of Adults   they may receive the eternal reward that you promise.

T HEN God remembered Rachel; God heard her prayer and
Genesis 30:22   made her fruitful.

M AY the One who blessed our mothers, Sarah, Rebekah,
Leah and Rachel, bless this child and keep her from all
harm. May her parents rear her to dedicate her life in faithful-
ness to God, her heart receptive always to the Law and the
Commandments. Then shall she bring blessing to her parents,
Jewish blessing   her people and all the world.

L ABAN had two daughters; the name of the elder was Leah, and the name of the younger was Rachel. Leah's eyes were lovely, and Rachel was graceful and beautiful. Jacob loved Rachel; so he said, "I will serve you seven years for your younger daughter Rachel." Laban said, "It is better that I give her to you than that I should give her to any other man; stay with me." So Jacob served seven years for Rachel, and they seemed to him but a few days because of the love he had for her.   Genesis 29:16–20

T HIS great season of grace is your gift to your family to renew us in spirit.
You give us strength to purify our hearts,
to control our desires,
and so to serve you in freedom.
You teach us how to live in this passing world
with our heart set on the world that will never end.   Roman rite

A LL that the saints counsel us about fleeing the world is clearly good. Well, believe me, our relatives are who cling to us the most.   Teresa of Avila
Sixteenth century

I N the last analysis, what does the word "sacrifice" mean? Or even the word "gift"? One who has nothing can give nothing. The gift is God's—to God.   Dag Hammarskjöld

B EING bound to an order and stability of observance, to a discipline of worship at set hours and fixed forms, is a celestial routine. Nature does not cease to be natural because of its being subject to regularity of seasons. Loyalty to external forms, dedication of the will, is itself a form of worship. The *mitzvot* [commandments] sustain their halo even when our minds forget to light in us the attentiveness to the holy. The path of loyalty to the routine of sacred living runs along the borderline of the spirit; though being outside, one remains very close to the spirit. Routine holds us in readiness for the moments in which the soul enters into accord with the spirit.

While love is hibernating, our loyal deeds speak. It is right that the good actions should become a habit, that the preference of justice should become our second nature; even though it is not native to the self. A good person is not one who does the right thing but one who is in the habit of doing the right thing.

Abraham Joshua
Heschel

Hosea 2:16, 18–20

O N that day, says the LORD, you will call me, "My husband." I will make for you a covenant on that day with the wild animals, the birds of the air and the creeping things of the ground; and I will abolish the bow, the sword and war from the land; and I will make you lie down in safety. And I will take you for my wife forever; I will take you for my wife in righteousness and in justice, in steadfast love and in mercy. I will take you for my wife in faithfulness, and you shall know the LORD.

T O love is good; love being difficult. For one human being to love another; that is perhaps the most difficult of all our tasks, the ultimate, the last test and proof, the work for which all other work is but preparation. For this reason [beginners] cannot yet know love: they have to learn it. . . . Learning-time is always a long, secluded time, and so loving, for a long while ahead and far on into life, is—solitude, intensified and deepened loneness for the one who loves. . . . it is a high inducement to the individual to ripen, to become something in oneself, to become world, to become world for oneself for another's sake, it is a great exacting claim, something that chooses one out and calls to vast things. Only in this sense, as the task of working at themselves ("to hearken and to hammer day and night") might young people use the love that is given them.

Rainer Maria Rilke

MAMA

YES—death done come in this here house. Done come walking in my house. On the lips of my children. You— what supposed to be my beginning again. You—what supposed to be my harvest. You—you mourning your brother?

BENEATHA

He's no brother of mine.

MAMA

What you say?

BENEATHA

I said that that individual in that room is no brother of mine.

MAMA

That's what I thought you said. You feeling like you is better than he is today? Yes? What you tell him a minute ago? That he wasn't a man? Yes? You give him up for me? You done wrote his epitaph too—like the rest of the world? Well, who give you the privilege?

BENEATHA

Be on my side for once! You saw what he just did, Mama! You saw him—down on his knees. Wasn't it you who taught me—to despise any man who would do that? Do what he's going to do?

MAMA

Yes—I taught you that. Me and your daddy. But I thought I taught you something else too—I thought I taught you to love him.

BENEATHA

Love him? There is nothing left to love.

MAMA

There is always something left to love. And if you ain't learned that, you ain't learned nothing. Have you cried for that boy today? I don't mean for yourself and the family 'cause we lost the money. I mean for him; what he been through and what it done to him. Child, when do you think is the time to love somebody the most; when they done good and made things easy for everybody? Well then, you ain't through learning—because that ain't the time at all. It's when he's at his lowest and can't believe in hisself 'cause the world done whipped him so. When you starts measuring somebody, measure him right, child, measure him right. Make sure you done taken into account what hills and valleys he come through before he got to wherever he is.

Lorraine Hansberry

I pray that Christ may dwell in your hearts through faith, as you are being rooted and grounded in love. I pray that you may have the power to comprehend, with all the saints, what is the breadth and length and height and depth, and to know the love of Christ that surpasses knowledge, so that you may be filled with all the fullness of God.

Now to him who by the power at work within us is able to accomplish abundantly far more than all we can ask or imagine, to him be glory in the church and in Christ Jesus to all generations, forever and ever. Amen.

Ephesians 3:17–21

A WAKE, O sleeper, rise from death,
And Christ shall give you light.
So learn his love—its length and breadth,
Its fullness, depth and height.

For he descended here to bring
From sin and fears release,
To give the Spirit's unity,
Which is the bond of peace.

There is one Body and one Hope,
One Spirit and one Call,
One Lord, one Faith and one Baptism,
One Father of us all.

Then walk in love as Christ has loved
Who died that he might save;
With kind and gentle hearts forgive
As God in Christ forgave.

For us Christ lived, for us he died
And conquered in the strife.
Awake, arise, go forth in faith,
And Christ shall give you life.

F. Bland Tucker

J ACOB said to Laban, "Give me my wife that I may go in to
her, for my time is completed." So Laban gathered together
all the people of the place and made a feast. But in the evening
he took his daughter Leah and brought her to Jacob, and he
went in to her. When morning came, he discovered it was
Leah! And Jacob said to Laban, "What is this you have done to
me? Did I not serve with you for Rachel? Why then have you
deceived me?" Laban said, "This is not done in our country—
giving the younger before the firstborn. Complete the week of
this one, and we will give you the other also in return for
serving me another seven years." Jacob did so.

Genesis 29:21–28

EVERY lapse into despair is a mortal wound inflicted by our own deliberate choice and will. If we refuse to abandon ourselves to the pit of indifference and despair, no evil spirit will have the slightest power over us. Even after we are wounded, we can still learn from this experience and become more courageous for the future if we repent with our whole heart. To save ourselves from every wound is not within our power, but whether we are to be mortal or immortal depends entirely upon ourselves. As long as we do not despair we shall not die.

Symeon
the New Theologian
Tenth century

EVERYTHING is for your sake, so that grace, as it extends to more and more people, may increase thanksgiving, to the glory of God.

So we do not lose heart. Even though our outer nature is wasting away, our inner nature is being renewed day by day. For this slight momentary affliction is preparing us for an eternal weight of glory beyond all measure, because we look not at what can be seen but at what cannot be seen; for what can be seen is temporary, but what cannot be seen is eternal.

2 Corinthians 4:15–18

JESUS told them a parable about their need to pray always and not to lose heart. He said, "In a certain city there was a judge who neither feared God nor had respect for people. In that city there was a widow who kept coming to him and saying, 'Grant me justice against my opponent.' For a while he refused; but later he said to himself, 'Though I have no fear of God and no respect for anyone, yet because this widow keeps bothering me, I will grant her justice, so that she may not wear me out by continually coming.'" And the Lord said, "Listen to what the unjust judge says. And will not God grant justice to the chosen ones who cry to God day and night? I tell you, God will quickly grant justice to them."

Luke 18:1–8

A T that very time there were some present who told Jesus about the Galileans whose blood Pilate had mingled with their sacrifices. He asked them, "Do you think that because these Galileans suffered in this way they were worse sinners than all other Galileans? No, I tell you; but unless you repent, you will all perish as they did. Or those eighteen who were killed when the tower of Siloam fell on them—do you think that they were worse offenders than all the others living in Jerusalem? No, I tell you; but unless you repent, you will all perish just as they did."

Then he told this parable: "A man had a fig tree planted in his vineyard, and he came looking for fruit on it and found none. So he said to the gardener, 'See here! For three years I have come looking for fruit on this fig tree, and still I find none. Cut it down! Why should it be wasting the soil?' He replied, 'Sir, let it alone for one more year, until I dig around it and put manure on it. If it bears fruit next year, well and good; but if not, you can cut it down.'"   Luke 13:1–9

F RAGMENTS of old sorrows float down to us through the ages: "The Galileans whose blood Pilate mixed with their sacrifices . . . the eighteen who were killed by a falling tower in Siloam . . ." That is all we know of the events. Did they have to do with armed rebellion? Were they both incidents of Roman oppression? Was the last just a dreadful accident? It does not matter. They are named simply as sorrows, and in the terse words are echoes and whispers of unconsoled weeping and unrelieved horror.

These words echo all the sorrows which assault us today, fragments of human pain calling out from short television accounts of starvation or quick headlines of brutal murders.

The way of Lent is not a way out of all this. The way of baptism, or of penance which is a return to our baptism, is not a way of distinguishing ourselves from others, making ourselves less sinners and so less liable to God's wrath.

On the contrary. Lent is a way into standing with the others. These suffering ones were not great sinners. Their lot is our lot. "You will all so perish." To repent is to acknowledge one's own need of life, to join with all those so desperately in need of life and to wait for God. That is the truth of baptism. That is the truth of penance as a return to baptism.

The way of Lent is the way of such repentance. We, all together, are to be Israel, the barren fig tree tended by the severe mercy of God until it bears fruit. The way of Israel in the desert was written down for us. And in that story of the desert we meet the burning truth of God, we encounter God's name which destroys all names—and we learn what that God does: "I have witnessed the affliction of my people . . . and have heard their cry."

This kind of repentance—standing with the suffering and sinful ones, turned toward God for life—is the way of Lent because it is the way of Jesus. The story of the cross is yet another among the dreadful fragments of sorrow. He is himself made the barren, and finally the uprooted fig tree. He is crucified with all the crucified. He is not distinguished from them. But just there he is God's mercy with us all. He is the burning bush itself. He is the name above all names. He is God hearing human sorrow and answering with life.

Gordon Lathrop

Graham Greene

YOU can't conceive, my child, nor can I or anyone, the appalling strangeness of the mercy of God.

O God, be merciful to me, a sinner.   Luke 18:13

A D te Rex summe, omnium Redemptor,
  oculos nostros sublevamus flentes:
exaudi, Christe, supplicantum preces.

Dextera Patris, lapis angularis,
via salutis, janua caelestis,
ablue nostri maculas delicti.

Tibi fatemus crimina admissa:
contrito corde pandimus occulta:
tua Redemptor, pietas ignoscat.

    Attende, Domine, et miserere,
    quia peccavimus tibi.

J ESUS our Savior, Lord of all the nations,
  Christ our Redeemer, hear the prayers we offer,
Spare us and save us, comfort us in sorrow.

Word of the Father, key-stone of God's building,
Source of our gladness, gate-way to the kingdom,
Free us in mercy from the sins that bind us.

Humbly confessing that we have offended,
Stripped of illusions, naked in our sorrow,
Pardon, Lord Jesus, those your blood has ransomed.

    Hear us, almighty Lord, show us your mercy   Latin hymn
    Sinners we stand here before you.   Tenth century

A SK rain from the LORD in the season of the spring rain,
from the LORD who makes the storm clouds,
who gives showers of rain to you,
Zechariah 10:1   the vegetation in the field to everyone.

N OW Elijah the Tishbite, of Tishbe in Gilead, said to Ahab,
"As the LORD the God of Israel lives, before whom I
stand, there shall be neither dew nor rain these years, except
by my word." The word of the LORD came to him, saying, "Go
from here and turn eastward, and hide yourself by the Wadi
Cherith, which is east of the Jordan. You shall drink from the
wadi, and I have commanded the ravens to feed you there."
So he went and did according to the word of the LORD; he
went and lived by the Wadi Cherith, which is east of the Jordan. The ravens brought him bread and meat in the morning,
and bread and meat in the evening, and he drank from the
wadi. But after a while the wadi dried up, because there was
1 Kings 17:1–7   no rain in the land.

L ET us know, let us press on to know the LORD,
whose appearing is as sure as the dawn;
God will come to us like the showers,
Hosea 6:1–3   like the spring rains that water the earth.

I T was a-thundering and lightning as if the heavens and earth
were a-coming together—so it seemed to me at that time.
And I felt it was just that I should be damned for sinning
against a just and holy God. I then felt a love mingled with
sorrow toward an insulted God, whom I had sinned against all
my days. While these thoughts with many more rolled against
my troubled breast, they covered me with shame, fear and
confusion to think of living all my days in sin and then dying
and being driven from the presence of a merciful and holy
God. It was more than I could bear.

I then thought, "I might as well go to Hell off my knees a-crying for mercy as anywhere else." So I kneeled at the head of the garret stairs, which was the first impression, and down I kneeled, and I cried and prayed to God with all my might and strength. The more I prayed, the worse I felt. My sins like a mountain reached to the skies, black as sack cloth of hair, and the heavens was as brass against my prayers, and everything above my head was of one solid blackness. And the fearful foreboding of my sudden destruction caused me to cry out in the bitterness of my soul, "Lord, I never will rise from my knees till thou for Christ's sake has mercy on my poor sinking soul or sends me to Hell." For I felt as though my soul had come into the chamber of death.

And in this moment of despair the cloud bursted, the heavens was clear, and the mountain was gone. My spirit was light, my heart was filled with love for God and all humankind. And the lightning, which was a moment ago the messenger of death, was now the messenger of peace, joy and consolation. And I rose from my knees, ran down the stairs, opened the door to let the lightning in the house, for it was like sheets of glory to my soul.

Rebecca Jackson
Nineteenth century

O NE day, one day
I was walking along;
Well, the elements opened
And the love come down,
Mount Zion.

Just talk about me
Just as much as you please;
Well, I'll talk about you
When I bend my knees,
Mount Zion.

On my journey now, Mount Zion,
On my journey now, Mount Zion.
Well, I wouldn't take nothin', Mount Zion,
For my journey now, Mount Zion.

African-American
spiritual

Sirach 35:26

G OD'S mercy is as welcome in time of distress
as clouds of rain in time of drought.

L ET works of mercy, therefore, be our delight, and let us be filled with those kinds of food that feed us for eternity. Let us rejoice in the replenishment of the poor, whom our bounty has satisfied. Let us delight in the clothing of those whose nakedness we have covered with needful raiment. Let our humaneness be felt by the sick in their illnesses, by the weakly in their infirmities, by the exiles in their hardships, by the orphans in their destitution, and by solitary widows in their sadness: in the helping of whom there is no one that cannot carry out some amount of benevolence. For no one's income is small whose heart is big, and the measure of one's mercy and goodness does not depend on the size of one's means. Wealth of good will is never rightly lacking, even in a slender purse. Doubtless the expenditure of the rich is greater and that of the poor smaller, but there is no difference in the fruit of their works where the purpose of the workers is the same.

Leo
Fifth century

Peter Chrysologus
Fifth century

M ERCY is to fasting as rain is to the earth. However much you may cultivate your heart, clear the soil of your nature, root out your vices and sow virtues, if you do not release the springs of mercy, your fasting will not bear fruit. When you fast a thin sowing of mercy will mean a thin harvest. When you fast what you pour out in mercy overflows into your barn. So do not lose by saving, but gather in by scattering.

THE quality of mercy is not strain'd;
  It droppeth as the gentle rain from heaven
Upon the place beneath. It is twice bless'd;
It blesseth him that gives and him that takes:
'Tis mightiest in the mightiest: it becomes
The throned monarch better than his crown:
His sceptre shows the force of temporal power,
The attribute to awe and majesty,
Wherein doth sit the dread and fear of kings:
But mercy is above this sceptred sway,
It is enthroned in the hearts of kings,
It is an attribute to God himself,
And earthly power doth then show likest God's
When mercy seasons justice.

William Shakespeare
Sixteenth century

WHILE I kept silence, my body wasted away
  through my groaning all day long.
For day and night your hand was heavy upon me;
    my strength was dried up
      as by the heat of summer.

Then I acknowledged my sin to you,
    and I did not hide my iniquity;
I said, "I will confess my transgression to the LORD,"
    and you forgave the guilt of my sin.

Psalm 32:3–5

YOU ask us to express our thanks by self-denial.
  We are to master our sinfulness and conquer our pride.
We are to show to those in need
    your goodness to ourselves.

Roman rite

L ET us pray for those of whose fall we have been told, that they may admit the gravity of their sin and realize that the remedy it calls for is anything but superficial. Let us pray that when they have received full forgiveness, they may do penance, and remembering their guilt, may decide to be patient for a time.

The church is still unsteady. May they not upset it altogether, its own members turning to persecution within it and crowning their many sins with the sin of trouble-making.

Cyprian of Carthage
Third century

J ESUS, Master, when we sin,
Turn on us thy healing face;
It will melt the offence within
    Into penitential grace.

Beam on our bewildered mind
    Till its dreamy shadows flee;
Stones cry out where thou hast shined,
    Jesus, musical with thee.

John Henry Newman
Nineteenth century

T HUS I create it good
    When God's
        Correction's understood,
Which is
        Not to destroy,
        But to reclaim,
    And t'cause me turn a new leaf o'er,
Making the scope of all my future aim
To reverence and glorify God's name.

Thus when our God will frown, if we weigh it
In judgment's scales, we make't a benefit.

Mildmay Fane
Seventeenth century

J ESUS told this parable to some who trusted in themselves that they were righteous and regarded others with contempt: "Two men went up to the temple to pray, one a Pharisee and the other a tax collector. The Pharisee, standing by himself, was praying thus, 'God, I thank you that I am not like other people: thieves, rogues, adulterers, or even like this tax collector. I fast twice a week; I give a tenth of all my income.' But the tax collector, standing far off, would not even look up to heaven, but was beating his breast and saying, 'God, be merciful to me, a sinner!' I tell you, this man went down to his home justified rather than the other; for all who exalt themselves will be humbled, but all who humble themselves will be exalted."

Luke 18:9–14

L IVE a humble, humble,
Humble yourselves, the bell's done rung!
Live a humble, humble,
Humble yourselves, the bell's done rung!
    Glory and honor! Praise King Jesus!
    Glory and honor! Praise the Lamb!

African-American
spiritual

O Lord,
    you have condemned the Pharisee
who justified himself by boasting of his works,
and you have justified the Publican who humbled himself
    and with cries of sorrow begged for mercy.
For you reject proud-minded thoughts,
but do not despise a contrite heart.
Therefore in abasement we fall down before you,
Jesus, who suffered for our sake:
grant us forgiveness and great mercy.

Byzantine Matins

THERE is no condition for forgiveness. But forgiveness could not come to us if we were not asking for it and receiving it. Forgiveness is an answer, the divine answer, to the question implied in our existence. An answer is answer only for one who has asked, who is aware of the question. This awareness cannot be fabricated. It may be in a hidden place in our souls, covered by many strata of righteousness. It may reach our consciousness in certain moments. Or, day by day, it may fill our conscious life as well as its unconscious depths and drive us to the question to which forgiveness is the answer.

Paul Tillich

I confess to almighty God,
and to you, my brothers and sisters,
that I have sinned through my own fault.
In my thoughts and in my words,
in what I have done,
and in what I have failed to do;
and I ask blessed Mary, ever virgin,
all the angels and saints,
and you, my brothers and sisters,
to pray for me to the Lord our God.

Roman rite

O Lord, God of the righteous,
you have not appointed repentance for the righteous,
for Abraham and Isaac and Jacob,
    who did not sin against you,
but you have appointed repentance for me,
    who am a sinner.
For the sins I have committed are more in number
    than the sand of the sea;
my transgressions are multiplied,
    O Lord, they are multiplied!

And now I bend the knee of my heart,
imploring you for your kindness.
I have sinned, O Lord, I have sinned,
and I acknowledge my transgressions.
I earnestly implore you,
forgive me, O Lord, forgive me!
Do not destroy me with my transgressions!
Do not be angry with me forever
    or store up evil for me;
do not condemn me to the depths of the earth.
For you, O Lord, are the God of those who repent,
and in me you will manifest your goodness;
for, unworthy as I am, you will save me
    according to your great mercy,
and I will praise you continually
    all the days of my life.
For all the host of heaven sings your praise,
and yours is the glory forever.
Amen.

Prayer of Manasseh
1:8–9, 11–15

A GAIN the throb of compassion rather than the breath of
consolation: the recognition of how long, how long is the
mourners' bench upon which we sit, arms linked in undeluded
friendship, all of us, brief links, ourselves, in the eternal pity.   Peter DeVries

Fourth
Week
of
Lent

Isaiah 66:10

R EJOICE with Jerusalem and be glad because of her, all you who love her.

T HE LORD, the God of their ancestors, brought up against the people the king of the Chaldeans, who killed their youths with the sword in the house of their sanctuary and had no compassion on young man or young woman, the aged or the feeble; God gave them all into his hand. All the vessels of the house of God, large and small, and the treasures of the house of the LORD, and the treasures of the king and of his officials, all these he brought to Babylon. They burned the house of God, broke down the wall of Jerusalem, burned all its palaces with fire and destroyed all its precious vessels. He took into exile in Babylon those who had escaped from the sword, and they became servants to him and to his sons until the establishment of the kingdom of Persia, to fulfill the word of the LORD by the mouth of Jeremiah, until the land had made up for its sabbaths. All the days that it lay desolate it kept sabbath, to fulfill seventy years.   2 Chronicles 36:17–21

T HERE are two times, says St. Augustine, one which is *now,* and is spent in the temptations and tribulations of this life; the other which shall be *then,* and shall be spent in eternal security and joy. In figure of these, we celebrate two periods: the time before Easter and the time after Easter. That which is before Easter signifies the sorrow of this present life; that which is after Easter, the blessedness of our future state. . . . Hence it is that we spend the first in fasting and prayer; and in the second we give up our fasting, and give ourselves to praise.

The church, the interpreter of the sacred scriptures, often speaks to us of two places, which correspond with these two times of St. Augustine. There two places are Babylon and Jerusalem. Babylon is the image of this world of sin, in the midst whereof we have to spend years of probation; Jerusalem is the heavenly country, where we are to repose after all our trials.   Prosper Guéranger

B Y the rivers of Babylon—
there we sat down and there we wept
   when we remembered Zion.
On the willows there
   we hung up our harps.
For there our captors
   asked us for songs,
and our tormentors asked for mirth, saying,
   "Sing us one of the songs of Zion!"

How could we sing the LORD'S song
   in a foreign land?
If I forget you, O Jerusalem,
   let my right hand wither!
Let my tongue cling to the roof of my mouth,
   if I do not remember you,
   if I do not set Jerusalem
Psalm 137:1–6   above my highest joy.

TWENTY-FIVE hundred years ago they were there, Jews exiled in Babylon, weeping into the river Euphrates. They could not drown their songs in the Euphrates—the river is too shallow—but their joys were flooded away. Singing the LORD'S song in a strange land, how they would have wished for a small round boat—a *kuphar*—to carry them safely up the river and back to the Holy Land. God had provided the willows lining the Euphrates. Perhaps God would provide also the skins: Hadn't Adam and Eve received their needed skins from the LORD? One can hear the faithful, choking on Zion's songs, groaning, ah! for a *kuphar*, a *kuphar* to take us home.

It is still the same. Along with our praises rises the plea that a boat will come our way, taking us from slavery back to our own free land. We beg for a ship to save us from the stormy wind by sailing us back to safety.

   Then were they glad because of the calm;
      the LORD brought them to the harbor
      they were bound for. Psalm 107

One boat has been granted, one *kuphar* for our Euphrates, one ark for our flood. We sit each week on its wooden benches, in that nave of ours, and sail home to God, in God.
Gail Ramshaw   For the *kuphar* God sends is the *kuphar* God is.

A s long as the community of Israel is in exile, the Divine Name remains incomplete.
                                                                           The Zohar

A LONG the banks where Babel's current flows
Our captive bands in deep despondence stray'd,
While Zion's fall in sad remembrance rose,
   Her friends, her children, mingled with the dead.   Early American hymn

W E are sojourners upon this earth; we are exiles and captives in Babylon, that city which plots our ruin. If we love our country, if we long to return to it, we ourselves must be proof against the lying allurements of this strange land and refuse the cup she proffers us, and with which she maddens so many of our fellow captives. She invites us to join in her feasts and her songs; but we must unstring our harps and hang them on the willows that grow on her river's bank, till the  signal be given for our return to Jerusalem. She will ask us to sing to her the melodies of our dear Sion: But how shall we, who are so far from home, have heart to "sing the song of the Lord in a strange land"? No, there must be no sign that we are content to be in bondage, or we shall deserve to be slaves for ever.
                                                                  Prosper Guéranger

W E are the pilgrims who must sleep every night beneath a new sky, for either we go forward to the new camp or the whirling earth carries us backward to one behind. There is no choice but to move, forward or backward. Forward to the clean hut, or backward to the old camp, fouled every day by the passers.
                                                                        Joyce Cary

IT was inch by inch that I sought the Lord,
Jesus will come by and by;
It was inch by inch that he saved my soul,
    Jesus will come by and by.

We'll inch and inch and inch along,
    Jesus will come by and by;
And inch by inch till we get home,
    Jesus will come by and by.

Oh, trials and troubles on the way,
    Jesus will come by and by;
But we must watch as well as pray,
    Jesus will come by and by.

Keep a-inching along, keep a-inching along,
    Jesus will come by and by.
Keep a-inching along, like a poor inchworm,
    Jesus will come by and by.

African-American
spiritual

TO improvise, first let your fingers stray
    across the keys like travelers in the snow:
each time you start, expect to lose your way.

You'll find no staff to lean on, none to play
among the drifts the wind has left in rows.
To improvise, first let your fingers stray

beyond the path. Give up the need to say
which way is right, or what the dark stones show;
they will show nothing till you lose your way.

And what the stillness keeps, do not betray;
the one who listens is the one who knows.
To improvise, first let your fingers stray;

out over emptiness is where things weigh
the least. Go there, believe a current flows
each time you start: expect to lose your way.

Risk is the pilgrimage that cannot stay;
the keys grow silent in their smooth repose.
To improvise, first let your fingers stray.
Each time you start, expect to lose your way.

Jared Carter

G UIDE me, O thou great Jehovah,
pilgrim through this barren land;
I am weak, but thou art mighty;
hold me with thy powerful hand;
bread of heaven, bread of heaven,
    feed me now and evermore,
    feed me now and evermore.

Open now the crystal fountain,
whence the healing stream doth flow;
let the fire and cloudy pillar
lead me all my journey through;
strong deliverer, strong deliverer,
    be thou still my strength and shield,
    be thou still my strength and shield.

When I tread the verge of Jordan,
bid my anxious fears subside;
death of death, and hell's destruction,
land me safe on Canaan's side;
songs of praises, songs of praises,
    I will ever give to thee,
    I will ever give to thee.

William Williams
Eighteenth century

F OR I am about to create new heavens
   and a new earth;
the former things shall not be remembered
   or come to mind.
But be glad and rejoice forever
   in what I am creating;
for I am about to create Jerusalem as a joy,
   and its people as a delight.
I will rejoice in Jerusalem,
   and delight in my people;
no more shall the sound of weeping be heard in it,
   or the cry of distress.

No more shall there be in it
   an infant that lives but a few days,
   or an old person who does not live out a lifetime;
for one who dies at a hundred years will be considered
      a youth,
for like the days of a tree shall the days of my people be,
Isaiah 65:17–20, 22   and my chosen shall long enjoy the work of their hands.

T HERE is no doubt about the mind of Christ here as the
   gospels reveal it: We must not think the service of God
can be subordinated to worldly purposes. If we seek first the
kingdom of God and God's justice, the new earth will be
added to us; if we give the earth and its fullness pride of place
in our lives and our hearts, we are idolaters and turn the house
of God into a den of thieves.

But it remains true that to live the life of God is, in fact, to find a
new earth, to see the earth as the habitation of glory, to see all
things in God and God in all things. We know the power that
things have to hurt us or give us joy because of their association with people we love: You love this place because one
you love made it heaven for you, you cannot go into this
room without pain because one you loved once lived in it. To
the eye of faith all the things that God has made have this

richness of association, and it should always be a cause for rejoicing, because the presence within them is an abiding presence and glory.

The pagan *lacrimae rerum,* the pathos of the passing of earthly beauty, is far from being the final word: In the eternal present all things abide, and behind the gleam of created beauty you sense the splendor of the divine. *Vere locus iste sanctus est:* truly this place is holy—the house of God and the gate of heaven.

So baptism affects more than our way of seeing the world; it gives us not just a new vision of the earth but a new earth.   Gerald Vann

C ITY of God, Jerusalem,
Where God has set such love;
Church of Christ that is one on earth
   With Jerusalem above:
Here as we walk this changing world
   Our joys are mixed with tears,
But the day will be soon when the Savior returns
   And his voice will banish our fears.

Look all around, Jerusalem,
   Survey from west to east;
Sons and daughters of God most high
   Are invited to the feast.
Out of their exile far away
   God's scattered family come,
And the streets will resound with the song of the saints
   When the Savior welcomes us home.   Christopher Idle

W E pray for these your servants
who have opened their ears and hearts
to your word.
Grant that they may grasp your moment of grace.

Do not let their minds be troubled
or their lives tied to earthly desires.
Do not let them remain
estranged from the hope of your promises
or enslaved by a spirit of unbelief.
Rather, let them believe in you,
whom the Father has established as universal Lord
and to whom he has subjected all things.

Let them submit themselves to the Spirit of grace,
so that, with hope in their calling,
they may join the priestly people
and share in the abundant joy of the new Jerusalem,
Rite of Christian
Initiation of Adults where you live and reign for ever and ever.

Galatians 4:26 J ERUSALEM is free,
and she is our mother.

I T is the day of all the year,
Of all the year the one day,
When I shall see my mother dear
And bring her cheer,
A-mothering on Sunday.

And now to fetch my wheaten cake,
To fetch it from the baker,
He promised me, for mother's sake,
The best he'd bake
For me to fetch and take her.

Well have I known, as I went by
One hollow lane, that none day
I'd fail to find—for all they're shy—
Where violets lie,
As I went home on Sunday.

George Hare Leonard

A Christian Lent can never be entirely sad. With the fourth Sunday the pent up spiritual joy in the true member of Christ bursts forth in anticipation of the Easter joy to come. "Rejoice, O Jerusalem, and come together all you that love her; rejoice with joy, you that have been in sorrow" (introit)— a note reechoed in the gradual and the offertory. The melody of the introit also is significantly that of the first Easter alleluia. This was the day when the catechumens were decked with roses and when roses were mutually exchanged. Thence comes the custom of the rose vestment.

Virgil Michel

B RIGHT sadness is the true message and gift of Lent. Little by little we begin to understand, or rather to feel, that the sadness of Lent is indeed "bright," that a mysterious transformation is about to take place in us. It is as if we were reaching a place to which the noises and the fuss of life, of the street, of all that which usually fills our days and even nights, have no access—a place where they have no power. All that which seemed so tremendously important to us as to fill our mind, that state of anxiety which has virtually become our second nature, disappear somewhere and we begin to feel free, light and happy. It is not the noisy and superficial happiness which comes and goes twenty times a day and is so fragile and fugitive; it is a deep happiness which comes not from a single and particular reason but from our soul having, in the words of Dostoyevsky, touched "another world." And that which it has touched is made up of light and peace and joy, of an inexpressible trust.

Alexander Schmemann

I was glad when they said to me,
"Let us go to the house of the LORD!"
Our feet are standing
    within your gates, O Jerusalem.
Jerusalem—built as a city
    that is bound firmly together.
To it the tribes go up,
    the tribes of the LORD,
as was decreed for Israel,
    to give thanks to the name of the LORD.
For there the thrones for judgment were set up,
    the thrones of the house of David.
Pray for the peace of Jerusalem:
    "May they prosper who love you.
Peace be within your walls,
    and security within your towers."
For the sake of my relatives and friends
    I will say, "Peace be within you."
For the sake of the house of the LORD our God,
    I will seek your good.

Psalm 122

REJOICE, O pilgrim throng!
Rejoice, give thanks, and sing!
Your festal banner wave on high,
    The cross of Christ your king.
Rejoice! Rejoice! Rejoice, give thanks, and sing!

With all the angel choirs,
    With all the saints on earth
Pour out the strains of joy and bliss,
    True rapture, noblest mirth.
Rejoice! Rejoice! Rejoice, give thanks, and sing!

Yet on and onward still,
 With hymn and chant and song,
Through gate and porch and columned aisle
 The hallowed pathways throng.
Rejoice! Rejoice! Rejoice, give thanks and sing!

Still lift your standard high,
 Still march in firm array,
As pilgrims through the darkness wend
 Till dawns the golden day.
Rejoice! Rejoice! Rejoice, give thanks, and sing!

At last the march shall end;
 The wearied ones shall rest;
The pilgrims find their home at last,
 Jerusalem the blest.
Rejoice! Rejoice! Rejoice, give thanks, and sing!

Edward H. Plumptre
Nineteenth century

W HY should we Christians feel joyful today? In the first place, this Sunday is a festival of spring. At least it was so in the early church. In olden times the first roses were brought to church for a blessing on this Sunday. (In Mediterranean lands spring comes much earlier.) Christians of former times lived much closer to nature than we do. When after the cold of winter spring comes to our land like a smiling youth, when in the fields God begins the miracle of multiplying bread, when God spreads a great table from which all creatures, the lowest to the highest, can eat their fill, when God lifts the white pall of winter from the earth and restores life in abundance to plants and animals—then Christians have cause to experience heartfelt joy, for they have a presentiment that Paradise is not far away.

Pius Parsch

THE freight of imagery, accumulated over a thousand years, bursts out in one blinding flash: For the Temple has become Jerusalem, and Jerusalem has become the Bride, and the Bride has become the Mystical Body, and the Lamb and his Wife are one. And everything is Christ, and everything is the Bride, and everything is the City where there is no temple, sun or moon, but only the Lamb who is its light. And the River flows back from the dawn of creation, and the Tree of Life returns from Eden, and the Gates of Jerusalem are not shut at all by day, and there is no night there. The tears, the sorrow, the crying and the pain are gone. It is all gardens, gallant walks and silver sounds:

> *There they live in such delight,*
> *Such pleasure and such play,*
> *As that to them a thousand years*
> *Doth seem as yesterday.*

By the drawing of the Mystery, the world has passed from its lostness and found him whom her soul loves. The Beloved comes leaping upon the mountains, skipping upon the hills. The time of the singing perpetually begins.

Vulnerasti cor meum, soror mea, sponsa; vulnerasti cor meum in uno crine colli tui. Si oblitus fuero tui, Jerusalem, oblivioni detur dextera mea. Adhaereat lingua mea faucibus meis si non proposuero Jerusalem in principio laetitiae meae.

Robert Farrar Capon　　Oh, Wow!

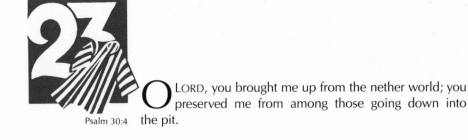

O LORD, you brought me up from the nether world; you preserved me from among those going down into the pit.

Psalm 30:4

J OSEPH told his brothers, "Look, I have had another dream:
the sun, the moon, and eleven stars were bowing down to
me." But when he told it to his father and to his brothers, his
father rebuked him, and said to him, "What kind of dream is
this that you have had? Shall we indeed come, I and your
mother and your brothers, and bow to the ground before
you?" So his brothers were jealous of him, but his father kept
the matter in mind.   Genesis 37:9–11

I N a dream, in a vision of the night,
when deep sleep falls on mortals,
    while they slumber in their beds,
then God opens their ears,
    and terrifies them with warnings,
that God may turn them aside from their deeds,
    and keep them from pride,
to spare their souls from the Pit.   Job 33:15–18

A N angel of the Lord appeared to Joseph in a dream and
said, "Joseph, son of David, do not be afraid to take Mary
as your wife, for the child conceived in her is from the Holy
Spirit. She will bear a son, and you are to name him Jesus, for
he will save his people from their sins." All this took place to
fulfill what had been spoken by the Lord through the prophet:
    "Look, the virgin shall conceive and bear a son,
        and they shall name him Emmanuel,"
which means, "God is with us." When Joseph awoke from
sleep, he did as the angel of the Lord commanded him.   Matthew 1:20–24

O H, Joseph being an old man, truly,
He married a maiden fair and free,
A purer maiden could no one see
Than who he took for his wife,
   his dearest dear.

The king of all powers was in Bethlehem born,
Who wore for our sakes a crown of thorn.
Then God preserve us both even and morn
For Jesus' sake,
   our dearest dear!

English carol
Fifteenth century

T HE words, the actions that hurt us most, often torment those who utter them, just as Joseph must have torn and rent his own mind and heart when he questioned if it were God's will that he should put his young love from him.

Even when this is not so, it is still so natural that it is almost inevitable that those with whom our lives are interlocked should be hurt and frightened when our surrender first takes place, for it will almost certainly reverse all of our values and all of theirs.

One newly converted to the faith, or reawakened to its meaning, is one who has fallen in love with God, and everyone in the house will feel the presence, the danger of the Divine Lover, whose demands may be uncompromising, may turn the complacency of the middle way topsy-turvy; the presence of the Lover who, to the beloved newly aware of God, will be utterly irresistible.

Christ is the Pied Piper to the human heart. He makes people become little children and suddenly turn the world they live in upside down, because they have been enchanted by him.

Caryll Houselander

ALL-PROVIDENT God,
the good things that grace this table
remind us of your many good gifts.

Bless this food,
and may the prayers of Saint Joseph,
who provided bread for your Son and food for the poor,
sustain us and all our brothers and sisters
on our journey toward your heavenly kingdom.

Blessing of a
St. Joseph's Table
Book of Blessings

JOSEPH, chaste and just, pray for us.
Joseph, prudent and brave, pray for us.
Joseph, obedient and loyal, pray for us.
Pattern of patience, pray for us.
Lover of poverty, pray for us.
Model of workers, pray for us.

Litany of St. Joseph

HOW beautiful will be the day when all the baptized
understand that their work, their job, is a priestly work,
that just as I celebrate Mass at the altar, so each carpenter
celebrates Mass at the workbench, and each metalworker,
each professional, each doctor with the scalpel, the market
woman at her stand, are performing a priestly office! How
many cabdrivers, I know, listen to this message there in their
cabs; you are a priest at the wheel, my friend, if you work with
honesty, consecrating that taxi of yours to God, bearing a message of peace and love to the passengers who ride in your cab.

Oscar Arnulfo Romero

JOSEPH went after his brothers and found them at Dothan. They saw him from a distance, and before he came near to them, they conspired to kill him. They said to one another, "Here comes this dreamer. Come now, let us kill him and throw him into one of the pits; then we shall say that a wild animal has devoured him, and we shall see what will become of his dreams." But when Reuben heard it, he delivered him out of their hands, saying, "Let us not take his life." Reuben said to them, "Shed no blood; throw him into this pit here in the wilderness, but lay no hand on him"—that he might rescue him out of their hand and restore him to his father. So when Joseph came to his brothers, they stripped him of his robe, the long robe with sleeves that he wore; and they took him and threw him into a pit. The pit was empty; there was no water in it.

Then they sat down to eat; and looking up they saw a caravan of Ishmaelites coming from Gilead, with their camels carrying gum, balm and resin, on their way to carry it down to Egypt. Then Judah said to his brothers, "What profit is it if we kill our brother and conceal his blood? Come, let us sell him to the Ishmaelites, and not lay our hands on him, for he is our brother, our own flesh." And his brothers agreed. When some Midianite traders passed by, they drew Joseph up, lifting him out of the pit, and sold him to the Ishmaelites for twenty pieces of silver. And they took Joseph to Egypt.

Genesis 37:17–28

TO you, O LORD, I cried,
and to the LORD I made supplication:
"What profit is there in my death,
    if I go down to the Pit?
Will the dust praise you?
    Will it tell of your faithfulness?
Hear, O LORD, and be gracious to me!
O LORD, be my helper!"

Psalm 29:8–10

FROM the night I seek thee early, O Lover of humankind: give me light, I pray thee, and guide me in thy commandments, and teach me, O Savior, to do thy will.

In night have I passed all my life: for the night of sin has covered me with darkness and thick mist. But make me, O Savior, a child of the day.

I confess to thee, O Christ: I have sinned, I have sinned like the brethren of Joseph, who once sold the fruit of purity and chastity.

As a figure of the Lord, O my soul, the righteous and gentle Joseph was sold into bondage by his brethren; but thou hast sold thyself entirely to thy sins.

O miserable and wicked soul, imitate the righteous and pure mind of Joseph; and do not live in wantonness, sinfully indulging thy disordered desires.

Joseph was cast into a pit, O Lord and Master, as a figure of thy burial and resurrection. But what offering such as this can I ever make to thee?

Byzantine Matins

COVER us, Lord, with your mercy. Be our protector and keep us from the dangers with which our sin surrounds us. Be our liberator and set us free.

Missal of Pius V

THIS is why the church has great conflicts: It accuses of sin. It says to the rich: Do not sin by misusing your money. It says to the powerful: Do not misuse your political influence. Do not misuse your weaponry. Do not misuse your power. It says to sinful torturers: Do not torture. You are sinning. You are doing wrong. You are establishing the reign of hell on earth.

Oscar Arnulfo Romero

THE brothers revealed their lack of humanity
    For enslaving Joseph, they sold him to the lawless;
But he placed all his faith in God,
    And he carried off the royal crown as he cried out:
"The Lord, our Savior, alone is mighty."
For if Isaac yielded to sacrifice by his father—
    Just one person commanding one—
        how shall I not endure
    The eleven brothers who enslave me?
Let us drain the streams of salvation
        that bring joy to the heart;
    We who are drunk with temperance,
        let us hasten to the cistern of Joseph.

Whoever drinks of its waters will never thirst;
    There, immortal water springs forth.
    Tell me how, when the cistern is entirely dry,
    Immortal water gushes forth?
Christ, whose type is prefigured in Joseph,
    Causes the water to flow as he did
        for the woman of Samaria.
    Then let us draw these waters with faith,
        for he is the Lord, our Savior,
        who alone is mighty.

Romanos
Sixth century

WHEN Reuben returned to the pit and saw that Joseph was not in the pit, he tore his clothes. He returned to his brothers and said, "The boy is gone; and I, where can I turn?" Then they took Joseph's robe, slaughtered a goat and dipped the robe in the blood. They had the long robe with sleeves taken to their father, and they said, "This we have found; see now whether it is your son's robe or not." He recognized it and said, "It is my son's robe! A wild animal has devoured him: Joseph is without doubt torn to pieces." Then Jacob tore his garments, and put sackcloth on his loins, and mourned for his son many days. All his sons and all his daughters sought to comfort him; but he refused to be comforted, and said, "No, I shall go down to Sheol to my son, mourning." Thus his father bewailed him.

Genesis 37:29–35

L ET us now add our lamentation to the lamentation of Jacob, and let us weep with him for Joseph, his wise and glorious son who was enslaved in body but kept his soul free from bondage, and became lord over all Egypt. For God grants a crown incorruptible.

Byzantine Matins

G OD did not spare his only Son, and God is not going to be soft on his adopted ones either.

The Hermitage Within

W ANTING to justify himself, a lawyer asked Jesus, "And who is my neighbor?" Jesus replied, "A man was going down from Jerusalem to Jericho and fell into the hands of robbers, who stripped him, beat him and went away, leaving him half dead. Now by chance a priest was going down that road; and when he saw him, he passed by on the other side. So likewise a Levite, when he came to the place and saw him, passed by on the other side. But a Samaritan while traveling came near him; and when he saw him, he was moved with pity. He went to him and bandaged his wounds, having poured oil and wine on them. Then he put him on his own animal, brought him to an inn and took care of him. The next day he took out two denarii, gave them to the innkeeper and said, 'Take care of him; and when I come back, I will repay you whatever more you spend.' Which of these three, do you think, was a neighbor to the man who fell into the hands of the robbers?" He said, "The one who showed him mercy." Jesus said to him, "Go and do likewise."

Luke 10:29–37

I will extol you, O LORD, for you have drawn me up,
and did not let my foes rejoice over me.
O LORD my God, I cried to you for help,
and you have healed me.
O LORD, you brought up my soul from Sheol,
restored me to life from among those gone down
to the Pit.

Psalm 30:1–3

a man who had fallen among thieves
lay by the roadside on his back
dressed in fifteenthrate ideas
wearing a round jeer for a hat

fate per a somewhat more than less
emancipated evening
had in return for consciousness
endowed him with a changeless grin

whereon a dozen staunch and leal
citizens did graze at pause
then fired by hypercivic zeal
sought newer pastures or because

swaddled with a frozen brook
of pinkest vomit out of eyes
which noticed nobody he looked
as if he did not care to rise

one hand did nothing on the vest
its wideflung friend clenched weakly dirt
while the mute trouserfly confessed
a button solemnly inert.

Brushing from whom the stiffened puke
i put him all into my arms
and staggered banged with terror through
a million billion trillion stars

e. e. cummings

I saw a stranger today.
I put food for him in the eating-place,
And drink in the drinking-place,
And music in the listening-place.
In the Holy Name of the Trinity
He blessed myself and my house,
My goods and my family.

And the lark said in her warble,
Often, often, often
Goes Christ in the stranger's guise
O, oft and oft and oft,
Goes Christ in the stranger's guise.   Irish rune

NOWHERE does the Torah say, Invite your guest to pray; but
it does tell us to offer a guest food, drink and a bed.   Jewish proverb

CHRIST, fowler of street and hedgerow
of cripples and the distempered old
—eyes blind as woodknots,
tongues tight as immigrants—
takes in his gospel net
all the hue and cry of existence.

Heaven, of such imperfection,
wary, ravaged, wild?

Yes. Compel them in.   Daniel Berrigan

JERUSALEM'S builder is the Lord,
Who gathers Israel's scattered people,
Who heals the brokenhearted,
    And binds up their painful wounds.   Psalm 147:2–3

JOSEPH could no longer control himself before all those who stood by him, and he cried out, "Send everyone away from me." So no one stayed with him when Joseph made himself known to his brothers. And he wept so loudly that the Egyptians heard it, and the household of the Pharaoh heard it. Joseph said to his brothers, "I am Joseph. Is my father still alive?" But his brothers could not answer him, so dismayed were they at his presence.

Then Joseph said to his brothers, "Come closer to me." And they came closer. He said, "I am your brother, Joseph, whom you sold into Egypt. And now do not be distressed, or angry with yourselves, because you sold me here; for God sent me before you to preserve life."

Genesis 45:1–5

THEN follows the ceremony of mutual forgiveness. The priest stands beside the *analogion,* and the faithful come up one by one and venerate the icon, after which each makes a prostration before the priest, saying: "Forgive me, a sinner." The priest also makes a prostration before each, saying the same words; and then the other receives his blessing and kisses his hand. Meanwhile the choir sings quietly the *irmoi* of the canon at Easter Matins. After receiving the blessing, the faithful also ask forgiveness of one another. When all have asked forgiveness, the priest says, "At the prayers of our holy ancestors . . . ," and so the service ends.

As described for Byzantine Vespers at the onset of Lent

GENUINE forgiveness is participation, reunion overcoming the powers of estrangement. And only because this is so does forgiveness make love possible.

Paul Tillich

JOSEPH said to his brothers, "Do not be afraid! Even though you intended to do harm to me, God intended it for good, in order to preserve a numerous people, as God is doing today."

Genesis 50:19–20

W HEREVER the waters flow, they bring health.   Ezekiel 47:9

A cup of rejoicing my Mother gave me,
'Tis full to the brim, 'tis full to the brim.
Sure these are the waters Ezekiel did see,
Wherein we can swim, wherein we can swim.

Pure love is the fountain and life is the stream
Our spirits doth fill, our spirits doth fill.
Here flowing, yea flowing, all souls to redeem,
For 'tis the Lord's will, for 'tis the Lord's will.   Shaker hymn

G OD our Mother,
Living Water,
River of Mercy,
Source of Life,
in whom we live
and move
and have our being,
who quenches our thirst,
refreshes our weariness,
bathes
and washes
and cleanses
our wounds,
be for us always
a fountain of life,
and for all the world
a river of hope
springing up in the midst
of the deserts of despair.   Miriam Therese Winter

A s Jesus walked along, he saw a man blind from birth. His disciples asked him, "Rabbi, who sinned, this man or his parents, that he was born blind?" Jesus answered, "Neither this man nor his parents sinned; he was born blind so that God's works might be revealed in him. We must work the works of the one who sent me while it is still day; night is coming when no one can work. As long as I am in the world, I am the light of the world." When he had said this, he spat on the ground and made mud with the saliva and spread the mud on the man's eyes, saying to him, "Go, wash in the pool of Siloam" (which means Sent). Then he went and washed and John 9:1–7   came back able to see.

T HE only reason for Jesus to mix clay with the spittle and smear it on the eyes of the blind man was to remind you that he who restored the man to health by anointing his eyes with clay is the very one who fashioned the first man out of clay, and that this clay that is our flesh can receive the eternal life through the sacrament of baptism.

You, too, should come to Siloam, that is, to him who was sent Ambrose of Milan   by the Father. Come and be baptized, it is time; come quickly, Fourth century   and you too will be able to say, *I was blind, and now I see.*

i N Just-
spring   when the world is mud-
luscious the little
lame balloonman

whistles   far   and wee

and eddieandbill come
running from marbles and
piracies and it's
spring

when the world is puddle-wonderful

the queer
old balloonman whistles
far   and   wee
and bettyandisbel come dancing

from hop-scotch and jump-rope and

it's
spring
and
   the

       goat-footed

balloonMan   whistles
far
and
wee
                                                e. e. cummings

THE jasmine behind my house has been completely ruined by the rains and storms of the last few days, its white blossoms are floating about in muddy black pools on the low garage roof. But somewhere inside me the jasmine continues to blossom undisturbed, just as profusely and delicately as ever it did. And it spreads its scent round the House in which you dwell, O God. You can see, I look after you, I bring you not only my tears and my forebodings on this stormy, grey morning, I even bring you scented jasmine. And I shall bring you all the flowers I shall meet on my way, and truly there are many of those. I shall try to make you at home always. Even if I should be locked up in a narrow cell and a cloud should drift past my small barred window, then I shall bring you that cloud, O God, while there is still the strength in me to do so. I cannot promise you anything for tomorrow, but my intentions are good, you can see.

Etty Hillesum

ILLE homo, qui dicitur Jesus, lutum fecit ex sputo, et linivit oculos meos, et modo video.

The one they call Jesus made mud from his spit and packed it on my eyes. And now I see!

Monastic liturgy

AMAZING grace! (how sweet the sound)
That saved a wretch like me!
I once was lost, but now am found,
Was blind, but now I see.

'Twas grace that taught my heart to fear,
And grace my fears relieved:
How precious did that grace appear,
The hour I first believed!

Through many dangers, toils, and snares,
I have already come;
'Tis grace has brought me safe thus far,
And grace will lead me home.

The Lord has promised good to me,
His word my hope secures:
He will my shield and portion be,
As long as life endures.

Yes, when this flesh and heart shall fail,
And mortal life shall cease,
I shall possess, within the veil,
A life of joy and peace.

The earth shall soon dissolve like snow,
The sun forbear to shine;
But God, who call'd me here below,
Will be for ever mine.

John Newton
Eighteenth century

L ORD Jesus,
you are the true light that enlightens the world.
Through your Spirit of truth
free those who are enslaved by the father of lies.

Stir up the desire for good in these elect,
whom you have chosen for your sacraments.

Let them rejoice in your light, that they may see,
and, like the man born blind whose sight you restored,
let them prove to be staunch and fearless witnesses
    to the faith,
for you are Lord for ever and ever.

*Rite of Christian
Initiation of Adults*

A S you have once given light
to the one blind from birth,
shine upon my soul, which does not see your light,
    O merciful Lord,
but lies buried in the darkness of sinful forgetfulness
and in the cares of this life.

Byzantine Matins

S ON of David, have pity on me!

What do you want me to do for you?

Lord, that I might see!

Monastic breviary

I want to walk as a child of the light.
I want to follow Jesus.
God set the stars to give light to the world.
The star of my life is Jesus.

I want to see the brightness of God.
I want to look at Jesus.
Clear sun of righteousness, shine on my path,
And show me the way to the Father.

I'm looking for the coming of Christ.
I want to be with Jesus.
When we have run with patience the race,
We shall know the joy of Jesus.

In him there is no darkness at all.
The night and the day are both alike.
The Lamb is the light of the city of God.
Kathleen Thomerson   Shine in my heart, Lord Jesus.

GIVE us, O God, the needs of the body,
Give us, O God, the needs of the soul;
Give us, O God, the healing balsam of the body,
Celtic prayer   Give us, O God, the healing balsam of the soul.

FASTING is a medicine. But like all medicines, though it be
very profitable to the person who knows how to use it, it
John Chrysostom   frequently becomes useless (and even harmful) in the hands of
Fourth century   those who are unskillful in its use.

OUR only health is the disease
If we obey the dying nurse
Whose constant care is not to please
But to remind of our, and Adam's curse,
And that, to be restored, our sickness must grow worse.

The whole earth is our hospital
Endowed by the ruined millionaire,
Wherein, if we do well, we shall
Die of the absolute paternal care
That will not leave us, but prevents us everywhere.   T. S. Eliot

YOUR children were not conquered
even by the fangs of venomous serpents,
for your mercy came to their help and healed them.   Wisdom 16:10

THE people spoke against God and against Moses, "Why
have you brought us up out of Egypt to die in the
wilderness? For there is no food and no water, and we detest
this miserable food." Then the LORD sent poisonous serpents
among the people, and they bit the people, so that many
Israelites died. The people came to Moses and said, "We have
sinned by speaking against the LORD and against you; pray to
the LORD to take away the serpents from us." So Moses prayed
for the people. And the LORD said to Moses, "Make a poisonous serpent, and set it on a pole; and everyone who is
bitten shall look at it and live." So Moses made a serpent
of bronze, and put it upon a pole; and whenever a serpent
bit someone, that person would look at the serpent of bronze
and live.   Numbers 21:5–9

THE serpent that Moses raised upon the staff
prefigured you, O Christ,
who was raised of your own will upon the cross:
for you have healed us from the poison of the evil one,
and in your love, you have drawn all your creation

Byzantine Matins   to yourself.

So that's it," Dr. Cameron said, greeting me at the elevator.
"Your daughter's temperature's been normal now for two
days, so it's probably let up. She's just walked in the hall
without any pains. She feels a lot better. Give it another day
and you can take her home. But anyhow, we've eliminated
everything serious."

That was the happiest moment of my life. Or the next several
days were the happiest days of my life. We could break bread
in peace again, my child and I. The greatest experience open
to us then is the recovery of the commonplace. Coffee in the
morning and whiskeys in the evening again without fear.
Books to read without that shadow falling across the page.
Carol curled up with one in her chair and I in mine. And the
bliss of finishing off an evening with a game of rummy and a
mug of cocoa together. And how good again to sail into Tony's
midtown bar, with its sparkling glasses, hitherto scarcely
noticed, ready to tilt us into evening, the clean knives standing
upended in their crocks of cheese at the immaculate stroke of
five. My keyed-up senses got everything: the echo of wood
smoke in Cheddar, of the seahorse in the human spine, of the
dogwood flower in the blades of an electric fan, or vice
versa. . . . But you can multiply for yourself the list of pleasures to be extorted from Simple Things when the world has
Peter DeVries   once again been restored to you.

'TIS the gift to be simple,
'tis the gift to be free,
'tis the gift to come down where we ought to be,
and when we find ourselves in the place just right,
'twill be in the valley of love and delight.
When true simplicity is gained,
to bow and to bend we shan't be ashamed,
to turn, turn, will be our delight,
till by turning, turning we come round right.　　　Shaker song

HAVE mercy on your people, Lord, and give us a breathing
space in the midst of so many troubles.　　　Missal of Pius V

CAN a mother forget her infant, be without tenderness for
the child of her womb?　　　Isaiah 49:15

JOSEPH died, and all his brothers, and that whole generation. But the Israelites were fruitful and prolific; they multiplied and grew exceedingly strong, so that the land was filled
with them.

Now a new king arose over Egypt, who did not know Joseph.
He said to his people, "Look, the Israelite people are more
numerous and more powerful than we. Come, let us deal
shrewdly with them, or they will increase and, in the event of
war, join our enemies and fight against us and escape from the
land." Therefore they set taskmasters over them to oppress
them with forced labor.　　　Exodus 1:6–11

W E got used to standing in line at seven o'clock in the morning, at twelve noon, and again at seven o'clock in the evening. We stood in a long queue with a plate in our hand into which they ladled a little warmed-up water with a salty or a coffee flavor. Or else they gave us a few potatoes. We got used to sleeping without a bed, to saluting every uniform, not to walk on the sidewalks, and then again to walk on the sidewalks. We got used to undeserved slaps, blows, and executions. We got accustomed to seeing piled-up coffins full of corpses, to seeing the sick amidst dirt and filth, and to seeing the helpless doctors. We got used to the fact that from time to time, one thousand unhappy souls would come here and that, from time to time, another thousand unhappy souls would go away.

Peter Fischl

WITH Amen on my lips, I approach
Your presence, Father. Not with fear,
But with a certain respectful fury.
I have very little time, as you well know.
Do you recognize my voice?
Must I reintroduce myself?
Ani Havazelet ha-Sharón.
Shoshanat ha-Amakim.
I am the Lily of Sharon, the Rose
Of the Valleys, Daughter of Zion.
I am that part of humankind you made
To suggest immortality.
You surely remember, Father? The part
That refuses death, that insists on you,
Divines your voice, guesses your grace.
And always you have heard my voice,
Always you have saluted me
With a rainbow, a raven, a plague, something.
But now I see nothing. This time you show me

Leonard Bernstein   Nothing at all.

M ANY books dictionaries
obese encyclopedias
but no one to give counsel

the sun is investigated
the moon the stars
I am lost

my soul
refuses consolations
sciences

I wander then by night
through the ways of the fathers

and behold
the little town of Bracław
among black sunflowers

this is the place which we deserted
this is the place which screams

it is Sabbath
as always on Sabbath
new heavens appear

—I am looking for you rabbi

—he is not here
say the Hasidim
—he is in the world of Sheol
—he had a beautiful death
say the Hasidim
—very beautiful
he all but arrived
from the one abode
to the other abode
all black
in his hand he had
a burning Torah

—I am looking for you rabbi

behind which block of heaven
have you concealed your wise ear

—my heart hurts me rabbi
—I have troubles

he would be able to counsel me
Rabbi Nachman
but how can I find him
Zbigniew Herbert   among so many ashes

INSIDE the kingdom of night I witnessed a strange trial. Three rabbis, all erudite and pious men, decided one winter evening to indict God for having allowed his children to be massacred. An awesome conclave, particularly in view of the fact that it was held in a concentration camp. But what happened next is to me even more awesome still. After the trial at which God had been found guilty as charged, one of the rabbis looked at the watch which he had somehow managed to preserve in the kingdom of night and said, "Ah, it is time for prayers." And with that the three rabbis, all erudite

Elie Wiesel   and pious men, bowed their heads and prayed.

O LORD, I cry out to you;
with my morning prayer I wait upon you.
Why, O LORD, do you reject me;
    why hide from me your face?
I am afflicted and in agony from my youth;
    I am dazed with the burden of your dread.
Your furies have swept over me;
    your terrors have cut me off.

They encompass me like water all the day;
  on all sides they close in upon me.
Companion and neighbor you have taken away from me;
  my only friend is darkness.   Psalm 88:14–19

G RANT, we beseech thee, almighty God, that we who are
chastised by fasting may rejoice also with true devotion,
that with our earthly affections being weakened, we may
more easily obtain the things of heaven.   Missal of Pius V

P HARAOH commanded all his people, "Every boy that is
born to the Hebrews you shall throw into the Nile, but you
shall let every girl live."

Now a man from the house of Levi went and married a Levite
woman. The woman conceived and bore a son; and when she
saw that he was a fine baby, she hid him three months. When
she could hide him no longer she got a papyrus basket for
him, and plastered it with bitumen and pitch; she put the child
in it and placed it among the reeds on the bank of the river. His
sister stood at a distance, to see what would happen to him.

The daughter of Pharaoh came down to bathe in the river,
while her attendants walked beside the river. She saw the
basket among the reeds and sent her maid to bring it. When
she opened it, she saw the child. He was crying, and she took
pity on him, "This must be one of the Hebrews' children," she
said. Then his sister said to Pharaoh's daughter, "Shall I go and
get you a nurse from the Hebrew women to nurse the child for
you?" Pharaoh's daughter said to her, "Yes." So the girl went
and called the child's mother. Pharaoh's daughter said to her,
"Take this child and nurse it for me, and I will give you your
wages." So the woman took the child and nursed it. When the
child grew up, she brought him to Pharaoh's daughter, and
she took him as her son. She named him Moses "because,"
she said, "I drew him out of the water."   Exodus 1:22 — 2:10

A WAY by the waters so blue,
The ladies were windin' their way,
And Pharoah's little daughter
Stepped down in the water
To bathe in the cool of the day.
Before it was dark,
She opened the ark,
And found a sweet infant was there.
Before it was dark,
She opened the ark,
And found a sweet infant was there.

And away by the waters so clear,
The infant was lonely and sad.
She took him in pity,
and thought him so pretty,
And it made little Moses so glad.
She called him her own,
Her beautiful son,
And sent for the nurse that was near.
She called him her own,
Her beautiful son,
And sent for the nurse that was near.

And away by the river so blue,
They carried the beautiful child
To his own tender mother,
His sister and brother,
Little Moses looked happy and smiled.
His mother so good
Done all that she could
To rear him and teach him with care.
His mother so good
Done all that she could
American folk ballad   To rear him and teach him with care.

THOU hast heard, my soul, of the basket of Moses: how he was borne on the waves of the river as if in a shrine; and so he avoided the bitter execution of Pharaoh's decree.

Thou hast heard, wretched soul, of the midwives who once killed in its infancy their own self-control: like great Moses, then, be suckled on wisdom.

The Great Canon of Lent

DO not fear, for I have redeemed you;
I have called you by name, you are mine.
When you pass through the waters, I will be with you;
   and through the rivers, they shall not overwhelm you.
For I am the LORD your God,
   the Holy One of Israel, your Savior.

Isaiah 43:2–3

ZION said, "The LORD has forsaken me,
my LORD has forgotten me."
Can a woman forget her nursing child,
   or show no compassion for the child of her womb?
Even these may forget,
   yet I will not forget you.

Isaiah 49:14–15

A mother may allow her child sometimes to fall, and to learn the hard way, for its own good. But because she loves the child she will never allow the situation to become dangerous. Admittedly earthly mothers have been known to let their children die, but our heavenly Mother, Jesus, will never let us, his children, die.

Julian of Norwich
Fourteenth century

M ARY modyr, cum and se:
Thi Son is naylyd on a tre.

His body is wrappyd all in woe,
Hand and fot; he may not go;
Thi Son, lady, that thou lovyst soo,
Nakyd is naylyd upon a tre.

Wan Johan this tale began to tell,
Mary wyld not lenger dwell
Tyl sche cam to that hyll
    Ther sche myht her owyn Son se.

"My swet Son, thou art me der;
Qwy have men hang thee here?
English carol Thi hed is closyd wyth a brier;
Fifteenth century   Qwy have men soo doo to thee?"

H AIL, fair star, that yieldest a ray of new light
whereby is blotted out
the shame of our race.

Thou art the flowery rod of Jesse:
thou art the true first spring flower,
bringing us our Jesus.

Thy virginal womb is the font of the garden,
the source of one
that is the water of life.

Thou art the font that givest forth oil,
yea, a dew sweet as honey;
for thou art all love.

Hence came to us the font
that washeth away the bitterness
and the stains of sin.

O Mother, whose heart was pierced
by the wounds of thy suffering Son,
show us a Mother's care and love;
and when the dread judgment comes,   Latin hymn
deliver us from punishment.   Cluny missal

THE Lord is believed to have been conceived on the 25th
day of March, upon which day he also suffered. So the
womb of the Virgin in which he was conceived, where no
mortal was ever begotten, corresponds to the new grave in
which he was buried, wherein no one was ever laid, neither   Augustine of Hippo
before him nor since.   Fourth century

CHRISTIANITY, it would seem, very early included the
incarnation among the themes of the total mystery of
Christ celebrated at Pascha, following the Passover tradition.
That incarnation theme was more theological than historical,
however, and before long the tolerable ambiguity of the time
of the incarnation was drawn to a sharper focus by early
christological controversy. The emerging understanding of
the incarnation as the taking of flesh by the preexistent Logos
directed attention from the baptism of Jesus, at which he was
acclaimed to be the divine Son, to the beginning of Jesus' life
as the beginning of the messianic mission, which would reach
its climax at Pascha. With that, then, the incarnation as it was
included in the themes of Pascha came to be understood as
the conception of the Lord, the annunciation, and that itself
defined the date of the nativity.   Thomas J. Talley

I N the sixth month the angel Gabriel was sent by God to a town in Galilee called Nazareth, to a virgin engaged to a man whose name was Joseph, of the house of David. The virgin's name was Mary. And he came to her and said, "Greetings, favored one! The Lord is with you." But she was much perplexed by his words and pondered what sort of greeting this might be. The angel said to her, "Do not be afraid, Mary, for you have found favor with God. And now, you will conceive in your womb and bear a son, and you will name him Jesus. He will be great, and will be called the Son of the Most High, and the Lord God will give to him the throne of his ancestor David. He will reign over the house of Jacob forever, and of his kingdom there will be no end." Mary said to the angel, "How can this be, since I am a virgin?" The angel said to her, "The Holy Spirit will come upon you, and the power of the Most High will overshadow you; therefore the child to be born will be holy; he will be called Son of God. And now, your relative Elizabeth in her old age has also conceived a son; and this is the sixth month for her who was said to be barren. For nothing will be impossible with God." Then Mary said, "Here am I, the servant of the Lord; let it be with me according to Luke 1:26–38   your word." Then the angel departed from her.

T HE threefold terror of love, a fallen flare
Through the hollow of an ear;
Wings beating about the room;
The terror of all terrors that I bore
The Heavens in my womb.

Have I not found content among the shows
Every common woman knows,
Chimney corner, garden walk,
Or rocky cistern where we tread the clothes
And gather all the talk?

What is this flesh I purchased with my pains,
This fallen star my milk sustains,
This love that makes my heart's blood stop
Or strikes a sudden chill into my bones
And bids my hair stand up?

William Butler Yeats

O my Lady, the holy Virgin Mary, thou didst confine the Unconfinable, and carry him whom none has power to sustain. What an unheard of thing for the potter to clothe himself in a clay vessel, or the craftsperson in a handicraft! What humility beyond words for the Creator to clothe himself in the body of a human creature!

Ethiopian prayer

G ABRIEL'S message does away
Satan's curse and Satan's sway,
out of darkness brings our day:
    So, behold, all the gates of heaven unfold.

He that comes despised shall reign;
he that cannot die, be slain;
death by death its death shall gain:
    So, behold, all the gates of heaven unfold.

Weakness shall the strong confound;
by the hands in grave clothes wound
Adam's chains shall be unbound:
    So, behold, all the gates of heaven unfold.

Latin carol
Sixteenth century

L ET in the wind,
Let in the rain,
Let in the moors tonight,

The storm beats on my window-pane,
Night stands at my bed-foot,
Let in the fear,
Let in the pain,
Let in the trees that toss and groan,
Let in the north tonight.

Let in the nameless formless power
That beats upon my door,
Let in the ice, let in the snow,
The banshee howling on the moor,
The bracken-bush on the bleak hillside,
Let in the dead tonight.

The whistling ghost behind the dyke,
The dead that rot in mire,
Let in the thronging ancestors
The unfulfilled desire,
Let in the wraith of the dead earl,
Let in the dead tonight.

Let in the cold,
Let in the wet,
Let in the loneliness,
Let in the quick,
Let in the dead,
Let in the unpeopled skies.

Oh how can virgin fingers weave
A covering for the void,
How can my fearful heart conceive
Gigantic solitude?
How can a house so small contain
A company so great?
Let in the dark,

Let in the dead,
Let in your love tonight.

Let in the snow that numbs the grave,
Let in the acorn-tree,
The mountain stream and mountain stone,
Let in the bitter sea.

Fearful is my virgin heart
And frail my virgin form,
And must I then take pity on
The raging of the storm
That rose up from the great abyss
Before the earth was made,
That pours the stars in cataracts
And shakes this violent world?

Let in the fire,
Let in the power,
Let in the invading might.

Gentle must my fingers be
And pitiful my heart
Since I must bind in human form
A living power so great,
A living impulse great and wild
That cries about my house
With all the violence of desire
Desiring this my peace.

Pitiful my heart must hold
The lonely stars at rest,
Have pity on the raven's cry,
The torrent and the eagle's wing,
The icy water of the tarn
And on the biting blast.

Let in the wound,
Let in the pain,
Let in your child tonight.   Kathleen Raine

THE eternal Father could not intend anything for the mother of the incarnate Son, without intending it for us too, and giving it to us in the sacrament of justification. For us too God eternally intended this saving grace from the beginning, in eternity, even though it was only effected in us after the beginning of our earthly, temporal life, in order that it might be plain that it is all God's grace, that nothing in our salvation belongs to us of ourselves. God has eternally kept eternal love in readiness for us too, so that in the moment that we call our baptism, God may come into the depths of our heart. For we too are redeemed, saved, marked with God's indelible seal. We too have been made the holy temple of God. In us, too, the triune God dwells. We too are anointed, hallowed, filled with the light and life of God. We too have been sent by God, from this beginning, into our life, that we too may carry the light of faith and the flame of love through this world's darkness, to the place where we belong, in God's eternal radiance, God's eternity.

Karl Rahner

LORD,
fill our hearts with your grace:
once, through the message of an angel
you revealed to us the incarnation of your Son;
now, through his suffering and death
lead us to the glory of his resurrection.

Angelus prayer

Sirach 45:1

DEAR to God and to all, Moses, whose memory is held in benediction.

To praise, that's it! Called to praise,
he came like ore out of the silence
of stone, Oh, his heart's a perishable press
of a wine that's eternal for us.

When he's in a godlike example's grip,
his voice isn't graveled by drought.
All turns vineyard, all turns grape,
ripened in his sensitive South.

Neither mould in the vaults of kings
nor a shadow that falls from the gods
makes a lie out of his praise.

He's one of the messengers who stays,
still extending bowls of glorious
fruit deep inside the doors of the dead.   Rainer Maria Rilke

Moses was keeping the flock of his father-in-law Jethro,
the priest of Midian; he led his flock beyond the
wilderness, and came to Horeb, the mountain of God. There
the angel of the LORD appeared to him in a flame of fire out of
a bush; he looked, and the bush was blazing, yet it was not
consumed. Then Moses said, "I must turn aside and look at
this great sight, and see why the bush is not burned up." When
the LORD saw that he had turned aside to see, God called to
him out of the bush, "Moses, Moses!" And he said, "Here I
am." Then he said, "Come no closer! Remove the sandals
from your feet, for the place on which you are standing is holy
ground." He said further, "I am the God of your father, the
God of Abraham, the God of Isaac, and the God of Jacob."
And Moses hid his face, for he was afraid to look at God.   Exodus 3:1–6

T HE boy stood there, straining forward, but the scene faded in the gathering darkness. Night descended until there was nothing but a thin streak of red between it and the black line of earth but still he stood there. He felt his hunger no longer as a pain but as a tide. He felt it rising in himself through time and darkness, rising through the centuries, and he knew that it rose in a line of men whose lives were chosen to sustain it, who would wander in the world, strangers from that violent country where the silence is never broken except to shout the truth. He felt it building from the blood of Abel to his own, rising and engulfing him. It seemed in one instant to lift and turn him. He whirled toward the treeline. There, rising and spreading in the night, a red-gold tree of fire ascended as if it would consume the darkness in one tremendous burst of flame. The boy's breath went out to meet it. He knew that this was the fire that had encircled Daniel, that had raised Elijah from the earth, that had spoken to Moses and would in the instant speak to him. He threw himself to the ground and with his face against the dirt of the grave, he heard the command. GO WARN THE CHILDREN OF GOD OF THE TERRIBLE SPEED OF MERCY. The words were as silent as seeds opening one at a

Flannery O'Connor   time in his blood.

I was determined that the fire shall not consume me, since you have given me your body and blood to feed me. I refuse to be carried off to hell, for you have given me baptism as a garment to clothe me. Grant me the dew of your grace, and in your mercy, Lord, forgive me my sins.

Rabbula of Edessa
Fifth century

W E are masters in our non-violent movement in disarming police forces, they don't know what to do. I've seen them so often. I remember in Birmingham, Alabama, when we were in that majestic struggle there, we would move out of the 16th Street Baptist Church day after day; by the hundreds we would move out. And Bull Connor would tell them to send the dogs forth and they did come; but we just went before the dogs singing, "Ain't gonna let nobody turn me round." Bull Connor next would say, "Turn the fire hoses on." And as I said to you the other night, Bull Connor didn't know history. He knew a kind of physics that somehow didn't relate to the transphysics that we knew about. And that was the fact that there was a certain kind of fire that no water could put out. And we went before the fire hoses; we had known water. If we were Baptist or some other denomination, we had been immersed. If we were Methodist, and some others, we had been sprinkled, but we knew water.

Martin Luther King, Jr.

THE LORD used to speak to Moses face to face, as one speaks to a friend.

Exodus 33:11

IN an alley between two shops, an old woman sat upon the ground; he could just see the rotting and discoloured face: it was like the sight of damnation. Then he heard the whisper, "Blessed art thou among women," and saw the grey fingers fumbling at the beads. This was not one of the damned: he watched with horrified fascination: this was one of the saved.

Graham Greene

LOOK at the Lord, and be radiant!
Do not let your face look ashamed.

Psalm 34:5

LOOK with favor, Lord, on your household. Grant that, though our flesh be humbled by abstinence from food, our souls, hungering after you, may be resplendent in your sight.

Missal of Pius V

F ASTING rewarded Moses with the sight of God.
Let our fasting, Christ our God,
win for us the joy of your great mercy.

Byzantine antiphon

B UT that Christ on this Crosse, did rise and fall,
Sinne had eternally benighted all.
Yet dare I almost be glad, I do not see
That spectacle of too much weight for mee.
Who sees God's face, that is selfe life, must dye;
What a death were it then to see God dye?

John Donne
Seventeenth century

T HROUGH the centuries down to our own day mothers
have made the sign of the cross in its original form, as
attested as far back as the third century and as now restored in
the baptismal liturgy: that is, with a single cross on the
forehead. Later on, these children may sign themselves with a
triple cross on forehead, mouth and breast, or may embrace
forehead, shoulders and heart in a single large sign of the
cross. In either case, the meaning is the same as when their
mothers signed them each night. But now these children will
be saying to themselves as it were: "I am baptized. Christ is my
Lord. I belong to Christ."

Balthasar Fischer

G O through the city, through Jerusalem, and put a mark on
the foreheads of those who sigh and groan over all the
abominations that are committed in it.

Ezekiel 9:4

N OWADAYS the sign of the cross normally calls to mind the gibbet to which Christ was nailed. But we have to ask ourselves whether this was the primary origin of the sign on the forehead in the primitive Christian community. It seems indeed that it was not, that in the beginning it was a matter of a sign that had a different significance. We have to notice that several ancient texts compare the sign of the cross with the letter *tau,* which in Greek had the form T. The fathers of the church themselves remark that the Book of Ezekiel declares that the members of the messianic community will be marked on their foreheads with the sign *tau. Tau,* the last letter of the Hebrew alphabet, signifies God, as does the Greek *omega.* In Christ's time the *tau* of the Hebrew alphabet was represented by the sign + or ×. It is in this form that we meet it in Palestinian ossuaries of the first century, and there we may possibly have the oldest Christian representation of the cross. It signified the name of God.

Jean Daniélou

W E should with a bundle of humility, as it were with a painter's brush dipped in the red blood of Christ, mark ourselves on every side, and on the lintel of our foreheads, with the letter *tau,* the sign of Christ's holy cross. And then will God himself, with his holy angels, pass by and kill and destroy for us those firstborn of the Egyptians, from the firstborn child of the king who sits on his throne, that is to say of pride, which is of all sins the prince, unto the firstborn child of the poorest captive slave, and that is covetousness.

Thomas More
Sixteenth century

A N unsealed treasure is at the mercy of thieves; a sheep without its brand is at the mercy of wolves. So the person without the *sphragis* is at the mercy of the devil.

Severian of Gabala
Fourth century

P AUL, when referring to the marks of Jesus on his own body, used an interesting Greek word: *stigma.* A *stigma* as we know it is a mark of disgrace or reproach—like the scarlet letter "A" that marked Hester Prynne as an adultress in Hawthorne's classic story of a stern and rigid morality of the Puritans in New England. In the Roman world of Paul's day, a slave who attempted to escape or steal from his or her master was marked with a red-hot branding iron. The resulting scar was called a *stigma,* and of course it was a mark of disgrace. But not all bodily marks were signs of reproach. It is said that people at that time proudly wore religious tattoos on their bodies, and these marks also were called *stigmas.* It is possible that the early Christians had themselves tattooed with symbols of their faith.

Joseph A. Hill

Rite of Christian Initiation of Adults

L ORD,
we have signed these catechumens
with the sign of Christ's cross.

Protect them by its power,
so that, faithful to the grace which has begun in them,
they may keep your commandments
and come to the glory of rebirth in baptism.

O NE day the king summoned his counselor and told him of his anguish: "I have read in the stars that all those who will eat of the next harvest will be struck with madness. What shall we do, my friend?"

"Nothing could be more simple, Sire," replied the counselor, "we shall not touch it. Last year's harvest is not yet exhausted. You have but to requisition it; it will be ample for you. And me."

"And the others?" scolded the king. "All the subjects of my kingdom? The faithful servants of the crown? The men, the women, the madmen and the beggars, are you forgetting them? Are you forgetting the children, the children too?"

"I am forgetting nobody, Sire. But as your adviser, I must be realistic and take all the possibilities into account. We don't have enough reserves, not enough to protect and satisfy everyone. There will be just enough for you. And me."

Thereupon the king's brow darkened, and he said: "Your solution does not please me. Is there no other? Never mind. But I refuse to separate myself from my people, and I don't care to remain lucid in the midst of a people gone mad. Therefore we shall all enter madness together. You and I like the others, with the others. When the world is gripped by delirium, it is senseless to watch from the outside: the mad will think that we are mad too. And yet, I should like to safeguard some reflection of our present glory and of our anguish too; I should like to keep alive the memory of this determination, this decision. I should like that when the time comes, you and I shall remain aware of our predicament."

"Whatever for, Sire?"

"It will help us, you'll see. And thus we shall be able to help our friends. Who knows, perhaps thanks to us, people will find the strength to resist later, even if it is too late."

And putting his arm around his friend's shoulder, the king went on: "You and I shall therefore mark each other's foreheads with the seal of madness. And every time we shall look at one another, we shall know, you and I, that we are mad."   Elie Wiesel

A LMIGHTY God, even while fasting disciplines us, may the spirit of these days bring us joy. Even as our love for this world grows less, may we more easily lay hold of heaven.   Missal of Pius V

Psalm 106:19   THEY made a calf in Horeb and adored a molten image.

YOU shall not make for yourself an idol, whether in the form of anything that is in heaven above, or that is on the earth beneath, or that is in the water under the earth. You shall not bow down to them or worship them; for I the LORD your God am a jealous God, punishing children for the iniquity of parents, to the third and fourth generation of those who reject me, but showing steadfast love to the thousandth generation Exodus 20:4–6   of those who love me and keep my commandments.

REMEMBER, O Lord, the catechumens of thy people: have mercy on them, confirm them in faith which is in thee. Cast out of their hearts remnants of every idolatrous worship; strengthen in their hearts thy law, thy fear, thy commandments, thy truth, thy holy precepts; grant them to know how to hold fast the words in which they have been instructed, so Gregory of Nazianzus   they be worthy of the washing of the new birth, for the Fourth century   remission of sins.

LORD our God,
you make known the true life;
you cut away corruption and strengthen faith,
you build up hope and foster love.

In the name of your beloved Son,
our Lord Jesus Christ,
and in the power of the Holy Spirit,
we ask you to remove from these your servants
all unbelief and hesitation in faith,
the worship of false gods and magic,
witchcraft and dealings with the dead,
the love of money and lawless passions,

enmity and quarreling,
and every manner of evil.

And because you have called them
to be holy and sinless in your sight,
create in them a spirit of faith and reverence,
of patience and hope,
of temperance and purity,
and of charity and peace.

*Rite of Christian
Initiation of Adults*

M OSES turned and went down from the mountain, carrying the two tablets of the covenant in his hands, tablets that were written on both sides, written on the front and on the back. The tablets were the work of God, and the writing was the writing of God, engraved upon the tablets. When Joshua heard the noise of the people as they shouted, he said to Moses, "There is a noise of war in the camp." But he said,

"It is not the sound made by victors,
or the sound made by losers;
it is the sound of revelers that I hear."

As soon as he came near the camp and saw the calf and the dancing, Moses' anger burned hot, and he threw the tablets from his hands and broke them at the foot of the mountain. He took the calf that they had made, burned it with fire, ground it to powder, scattered it on the water, and made the Israelites drink it.

Exodus 32:15–20

O UR immaturity and carelessness make light
of your law, O Lord,
and our sins disfigure our lives.
We fall before you in sorrow, O Savior,
and we implore you:
Create in us a pure heart, and in our bellies
a new and constant spirit,
and before we die, O Lord,
enable us to mend our ways and turn to you.

Byzantine prayer

W HEN the Stranger says:
"What is the meaning of this city?"
Do you huddle close together because you love each other?
What will you answer? "We all dwell together
to make money from each other"? or "This is community"?
And the Stranger will depart and return to the desert.
O my soul, be prepared for the coming of the Stranger,
Be prepared for him who knows how to ask questions.
   O weariness of those who turn from GOD
To the grandeur of your mind and the glory of your action,
To arts and inventions and daring enterprises,
To schemes of human greatness thoroughly discredited,
Binding the earth and the water to your service,
Exploiting the seas and developing the mountains,
Dividing the stars into common and preferred,
Engaged in devising the perfect refrigerator,
Engaged in working out a rational morality,
Engaged in printing as many books as possible,
Plotting of happiness and flinging empty bottles,
Turning from your vacancy to fevered enthusiasm
For nation or race or what you call humanity;
Though you forget the way to the Temple,
There is one who remembers the way to your door:
Life you may evade, but Death you shall not.

T. S. Eliot   You shall not deny the Stranger.

I F life can be made worthwhile, death will not matter at all;
for life can be good, but it is not and cannot be an absolute,
any more than anything else in this world. To make life into an
absolute is to exchange it for death-in-life, because, like every
other temporal absolute, life takes revenge on those who

Dorothy Sayers   make it a god.

CLEANSE your hands, you sinners;
purify your hearts, you backsliders.

James 4:8

I would not be a backslider,
And I'll tell you the reason why;
'Cause if my Lord should call on me,
I wouldn't be ready to die.

> There's plenty good room, plenty good room,
> Good room in my Father's kingdom.
> Plenty good room, plenty good room,
> Why don't you choose your seat and sit down?

African-American
spiritual

ALONG with our ancestors, we have sinned;
Doing injustice, distorting your way.
Our ancestors, even in Egypt,
    Did not comprehend your wonders.
They forgot your great fidelity,
    Refusing to trust you beside the Red Sea.
And yet, to show who you are, you saved them,
    To demonstrate your power.
You rebuked the Red Sea, and it drained away;
    You led them through deeps as though through a desert.
You redeemed them from those who hated them,
    And saved them from the grip of their foes.
The waters buried their oppressors.
    Not a single one survived.
Then they trusted in your word;
    Then they sang your praise.
But how quickly they forgot your deeds,
    Impatient with your intentions.
In the wilderness they nursed their cravings,
    And tested you, O God, in the desert.
You gave to them what they asked,

Freeing their stomachs from hunger.
And then, at Horeb, they made the calf,
And bowed in worship before a statue.
They exchanged the God who was their glory,
Psalm 106:6–15, 19–20   For the shape of a bull that feeds on hay.

R ESH Lakish said: "God says, 'In the hour when I conquer,
I suffer loss, but in the hour when I am conquered, I gain. I
conquered at the generation of the flood, but I lost, for I destroyed creation. So it was with the generation of the Tower of
Babel, and with the people of Sodom. But when the golden calf
was made, Moses conquered me, and I gained all creation. So
The Talmud   I acquit all my creatures so that I may not suffer loss.'"

D EAR candidates, you have set out toward your baptism.
You have answered God's call and been helped by
grace; you have decided to serve and worship God alone
and the one God has sent, Jesus Christ. Since you have made
this choice, now is the time to renounce publicly those
powers that are not of God and those forms of worship that
do not rightly honor God. Are you, therefore, resolved to
Rite of Christian   remain loyal to God and to the Christ and never to serve
Initiation of Adults   ungodly powers?

M ANY live as enemies of the cross of Christ; I have often
told you of them, and now I tell you even with tears.
Their end is destruction; their god is the belly; and their glory
Philippians 3:18–19   is in their shame.

I heard these words spoken by that spellbinding tree:
"I remember it yet, it was years ago,
borne on warriors' shoulders I was set on a hill
and fixed there by foes. I then saw humanity's Lord
hasten boldhearted to ascend upon me.
I did not then dare against the decree of the Lord
to bend or to break, though I beheld trembling
the surface of the earth. Surely I was able
to fell those foes; yet I stood fast.
The young hero stripped himself, he, God almighty,
strong and stouthearted. He ascended the hated gallows,
dauntless in the sight of many, to redeem humankind.

The Dream of the Rood
Eighth century

L ET me explain what my office is and how I am fulfilling it. I study the word of God to be read on Sunday. I look around me, at my people. I use this word to shed light on my surroundings, and I make a synthesis so as to be able to convey the word to the people and make them the light of the world, a people who allow themselves to be guided by principles and not by the earth's idolatries.

Naturally, the idols and idolatries of the earth are irritated by this word and they would like very much to remove it, to silence it, to kill it. Let happen what God wills, but God's word, as St. Paul said, is not tied down. There will be prophets, whether priests or lay people—there already are, in abundance —to understand what God wants to do through the word for our people.

Oscar Arnulfo Romero

R EMEMBER Jesus Christ, raised from the dead, a descendant of David—that is my gospel, for which I suffer hardship, even to the point of being chained like a criminal. But the word of God is not chained.

2 Timothy 2:8–9

Y OU can lock up the bold ones,
    Go and lock up your bold ones and hold them in tow.
You can stifle all adventure for a century or so.
Smother hope before it's risen, watch it wizen like a gourd.
But you cannot imprison the Word of the Lord.

No, you cannot imprison the Word of the Lord.

For the Word,
For the Word was at the birth of the beginning;
It made the heavens and the earth and set them spinning,
And for several million years
It's withstood all our forums and fine ideas:
It's been rough,
It's been rough but it appears to be winning!

There are people who doubt it,
There are people who doubt it and shout it out loud,
There are vocal local yokels who we know collect a crowd.
They can fashion a rebuttal that's as subtle as a sword,
But they're never gonna scuttle the Word of the Lord.

No, they're never gonna scuttle the Word of the Lord.

All you big men of merit,
All you big men of merit who ferret out flaws,
You rely on our compliance with your science
        and your laws.
Find the freedom to demolish while you polish
        some award,
But you cannot abolish the Word of the Lord.

No, you cannot abolish the Word of the Lord.

For the Word,
For the Word created mud and got it going.
It filled our empty brains with blood and set it flowing.
And for thousands of regimes
It's endured all our follies and fancy schemes.
It's been tough,
It's been tough, and yet it seems to be growing!

O you people of power,
O you people of power, your hour is now.
You may plan to rule forever, but you never do somehow.
So we wait in silent treason until reason is restored,
And we wait for the season of the Word of the Lord.

We await the season of the Word of the Lord.

Stephen Schwartz and
Leonard Bernstein

B EHOLD it is a time of war,
And we have been enlisting,
Emmanuel we're fighting for,
And Satan we're resisting.

We have not in this war begun
To turn our backs as traitors,
But we will all unite as one
Against our carnal natures!

Shaker hymn

T HE story is told that Moses was met by a group of Hebrews
when he came back down the mountain the second time,
after the first tablets of the commandments had been broken.
When he got near enough, they asked him how it went this
time. "Not too well," he replied. "It was tough bargaining. We
get the milk and honey, but the anti-adultery clause stays."

Lawrence E. Mick

I need to point out that God was first experienced by the
Israelites in the event of the Exodus. That was how they
came into contact with God. They were at the time just a
rabble of slaves. They did not encounter God in some religious event such as a sacrifice or at worship. God was
revealed in helping them to escape from bondage. . . . And
when God redeemed us in our Lord and Savior Jesus Christ, it
was not through a religious event. No, it was through an act of
execution, used against common criminals.

Desmond Tutu

A lamb alone bears willingly
Sin's crushing weight for sinners;
He carries guilt's enormity,
Dies shorn of all his honors.
He goes to slaughter, weak and faint,
Is led away with no complaint
His spotless life to offer.
He bears the stripes, the wrath, the lies,
The mockery, and yet replies,
"Willing all this I suffer."

This lamb is Christ, our soul's great friend,
The Lamb of God, our Savior,
Whom God the Father chose to send
Our rebel guilt to cover.
"Go down, my Son," the Father said,
"To free my children from their dread
Of death and condemnation.
The wrath of stripes are hard to bear,
But in your death they all can share
The joy of your salvation!"

"Yes, Father, yes, most willingly
I bear what you command me;
My will conforms to your decree,
I risk what you have asked me."
O wondrous love, what have you done?
The Father offers up his Son,
The Son, content, agreeing!
O Love, how strong you are to save,
To put God's Son into his grave,
All people thereby freeing!

Then, when we come before God's throne,
This little lamb shall lead us;
His righteousness shall be our crown,
His innocence precede us.
His grace our dress of royalty;

His all-forgiving loyalty
Unites us with our Father,
Where we shall stand at Jesus' side,
His church, redeemed and glorified,   Paul Gerhardt
Where all his faithful gather!   Seventeenth century

I was like a gentle lamb
led to the slaughter.
And I did not know it was against me
    that they devised schemes, saying,
"Let us destroy the tree with its fruit,
    let us cut him off from the land of the living,
    so that his name will no longer be remembered!"   Jeremiah 11:19

GOD in heaven, you have helped my life to grow like a
tree. Now something has happened. Satan, like a bird,
has carried in one twig of his own choosing after another.
Before I knew it he had built a dwelling place and was living in
it. Tonight, my Father, I am throwing out both the bird and
the nest.   Nigerian prayer

ALMIGHTY God, you alone can bring into order the unruly
wills and affections of sinners: Grant your people grace
to love what you command and desire what you promise;
that, among the swift and varied changes of the world, our
hearts may surely there be fixed where true joys are to be
found; through Jesus Christ our Lord, who lives and reigns   *Book of*
with you and the Holy Spirit, one God, now and for ever.   *Common Prayer*

Philippians 3:10

I wish to know Christ and the power flowing from his resurrection; likewise to know how to share in his sufferings by being formed into the pattern of his death.

LET us lie in wait for the righteous,
because they are inconvenient to us
    and oppose our actions;
they reproach us for sins against the law,
and accuse us of sins against our training.
They profess to have knowledge of God,
and call themselves children of the Lord.
They became to us a reproof of our thoughts;
the very sight of them is a burden to us,
because their manner of life is unlike that of others,
and their ways are strange.
We are considered by them as something base,
and they avoid our ways as unclean;
they call the last end of the righteous happy,
and boast that God is their father.
Let us see if their words are true,
and let us test what will happen at the end of their lives;
for if the righteous are God's children, God will help them,
and will deliver them from the hand of their adversaries.
Let us test them with insult and torture,
so that we may find out how gentle they are,
and make trial of their forbearance.
Let us condemn them to a shameful death,
Wisdom 2:12–20   for, according to what they say, they will be protected.

J ESUS' words and his life reflect the same spirit which we believe we see in Job, in Jeremiah, in the Servant of the Lord: that there is no answer to the problem of evil, and no way to meet evil in the concrete, except suffering and death. We have seen people in all the ages try to shake off the burden by the most varied and ingenious devices, and they have all failed. Jesus alone came and said: Take up your cross. If you wish to live, die. If you wish to find joy, suffer. He did not explain it; he simply lived that way. If there were a better answer to the problem, if there were a better way to meet it, it is hard to think that the Incarnate God would not have chosen it. He did not make evil easy to understand or easy to bear; he showed only that it is possible to live with it, and to live well, to live heroically, without doing anything about evil except to suffer it. This is the mystery of the Servant, the mystery of the life and death of Jesus, that it is in yielding to evil, in becoming its victim, in being consumed by it, that you have your only hope of overcoming it; and, by the solidarity which links Jesus with all and all with each other, this victory over evil can be communicated to others who are ignorant of what happens on their behalf.

John L. McKenzie

D IDST thou not make us one,
That we might one remain,
Together travel on,
And bear each other's pain;
Till all thy utmost goodness prove,
And rise renewed in perfect love?

Then let us ever bear
The blessed end in view,
And join, with mutual care,
To fight our passage through;
And kindly help each other on,
Till all receive the starry crown.

Charles Wesley
Eighteenth century

PILATE released Barabbas for them; and after flogging Jesus, he handed him over to be crucified. Then the soldiers of the governor took Jesus into the governor's headquarters and they gathered the whole cohort around him. They stripped him and put a scarlet robe on him, and after twisting some thorns into a crown, they put it on his head. They put a reed in his right hand and knelt before him and mocked him, saying, "Hail, King of the Jews!" They spat on him, and took the reed and struck him on the head. After mocking him, they stripped him of the robe and put his own clothes on him. Then they led him away to crucify him.

Matthew 27:26–31

IT is curious that people who are filled with horrified indignation whenever a cat kills a sparrow can hear that story of the killing of God told Sunday after Sunday and not experience any shock at all.

Dorothy Sayers

THE church's good name is not a matter of being on good terms with the powerful. The church's good name is a matter of knowing that the poor regard the church as their own, of knowing that the church's life on earth is to call on all, on the rich as well, to be converted and be saved alongside the poor, for they are the only ones called blessed.

Oscar Arnulfo Romero

Ignatius of Antioch
Second century

THE greatness of Christianity lies in its being hated by the world, not in its being convincing to it.

A TONEMENT means quite literally "to make one," but this reconciliation is costly because its path is through the suffering of the cross.

There is dying that goes with unity. There is pain that goes with giving up swords and spears, and living with pruning hooks and plows. There is pain and death and vulnerability that come with living in the world defenseless, but in that way comes unity.

The church has always been clear that as the body of Christ its life must be cruciform. Thus, if we are to make *shalom,* following Christ, it cannot be at the level of lowest risk. It will require becoming vulnerable to the pain of the world. It will require a willingness to die.

Bruce C. Birch and
Larry Rasmussen

A LAS! and did my Savior bleed,
And did my sov'reign die?
Would he devote that sacred head
For sinners such as I?

Was it for sins that I had done,
He groaned upon the tree?
Amazing pity, grace unknown,
And love beyond degree!

Well might the sun in darkness hide
And shut its glories in,
When God, the mighty maker, died
For God's own creatures' sin.

Thus might I hide my blushing face
While the dear cross appears,
Dissolve my heart in thankfulness,
And melt my eyes to tears.

But tears of grief cannot repay
The debt of love I owe;
Here, Lord, I give myself away:
'Tis all that I can do.

Isaac Watts
Eighteenth century

W HILE Peter was below in the courtyard, one of the servant-girls of the high priest came by. When she saw Peter warming himself, she stared at him and said, "You also were with Jesus, the man from Nazareth." But he denied it, saying, "I do not know or understand what you are talking about." And he went out into the forecourt. Then the cock crowed. And the servant-girl, on seeing him, began again to say to the bystanders, "This man is one of them." But again he denied it. Then after a little while the bystanders again said to Peter, "Certainly you are one of them, for you are a Galilean." But he began to curse, and he swore an oath, "I do not know this man you are talking about." At that moment the cock crowed for the second time. Then Peter remembered that Jesus had said to him, "Before the cock crows twice, you will deny me three times." And he broke down and wept.

Mark 14:66–72

O Christ, who art the light and day,
Thou drivest night and gloom away:
O Light of light, whose word doth show
The light of heav'n to us below.

O Lord, remember us who bear
The burden of the flesh we wear;
Thou, who dost o'er our soul defend,
Be with us even to the end.

Robert Whyte
Sixteenth century

W E can of course shake off the burden which is laid upon us, but only find that we have a still heavier burden to carry—a yoke of our own choosing, the yoke of our self. But Jesus invites all who travail and are heavy laden to throw off their own yoke and take his yoke upon them—and his yoke is easy, and his burden is light. The yoke and the burden of Christ are his cross.

Dietrich Bonhoeffer

A BSTAINING from the passions,
let us for the Lord's sake crucify our flesh;
by our life in Christ,
let us all show that the pride of the flesh is dead!   Byzantine Matins

H OW easy it is to hate oneself! True grace is to forget oneself. Yet if pride could die in us, the supreme grace would
be to love oneself in all simplicity—as one would love one of
those who themselves have suffered and loved in Christ.   Georges Bernanos

I T is certain that the fathers did well to use such lenience in
their desire to establish us in the habit of fasting. As we
know, we could proclaim a fast throughout the whole year,
and no one would pay any attention. But now, with a set time
for fasting of only forty days, even the most sluggish need no
exhortation to rouse themselves to undergo it. When someone asks you why you fast, you should not answer: because of
the Passover, or because of the cross. Neither of these is the reason for our fasting. We fast because of our sins, since we are
preparing to approach the sacred mysteries. Moreover, the
Christian Passover is a time for neither fasting nor mourning,
but for great joy, since the cross destroyed sin and made
expiation for the whole world. It reconciled ancient enmities
and opened the gates of heaven. It made friends of those who
had been filled with hatred, restoring them to the citizenship
of heaven. Through the cross our human nature has been set
at the right hand of the throne of God, and we have been
granted countless good things besides. Therefore we must not
give way to mourning or sadness; we must rejoice greatly   John Chrysostom
instead over all these blessings.   Fourth century

WHEN I survey the wondrous cross
     where the young Prince of Glory died,
my richest gain I count but loss,
   and pour contempt on all my pride.

Forbid it, Lord, that I should boast,
   save in the cross of Christ, my God:
all the vain things that charm me most,
   I sacrifice them to his blood.

See, from his head, his hands, his feet,
   sorrow and love flow mingled down!
Did e'er such love and sorrow meet,
   or thorns compose so rich a crown?

Were the whole realm of nature mine,
   that were an offering far too small;
love so amazing, so divine,
   demands my soul, my life, my all.

Isaac Watts
Eighteenth century

THE whole of the world which Jesus wills to draw to himself
     comes into the reality of the cross. The world is dependent
on the gravitation of this body, which inertia is causing to sink
lower and lower. The passion of Christ crucified resides in this
gravitation.

Karol Wojtyła

THE waves of death were all around me,
     The floods of destruction terrified me.
The bonds of Hades were looped about me,
   The snares of imminent death.
In my peril I cried out, "Lord!"
   I called for help to my God.
From your palace you heard my cry;
   My call for help came to your ears.

Psalm 18:4–7

A LL is in an enormous dark
Drowned. O pity and indignation!
  Manshape, that shone
Sheer off, disseveral, a star,
    death blots black out; nor mark
  Is any of us at all so stark
But vastness blurs and time beats level.
    Enough! the Resurrection,
A heart's-clarion! Away grief's gasping,
    joyless days' dejection.
  Across my foundering deck shone
A beacon, an eternal beam.
    Flesh fade, and mortal trash
Fall to the residuary worm;
    world's wildfire, leave but ash:
  In a flash, at a trumpet crash,
I am all at once what Christ is,
    since he was what I am, and
This Jack, joke, poor potsherd,
    patch, matchwood, immortal diamond,
  Is immortal diamond.

Gerard Manley Hopkins
Nineteenth century

F ATHER,
  source of all life,
in giving life to the living you seek out the image
    of your glory
and in raising the dead you reveal your unbounded power.

Rescue these elect from the tyranny of death,
for they long for new life through baptism. . . .

Place them under the reign of your beloved Son,
that they may share in the power of his resurrection
and give witness to your glory before all.

Rite of Christian
Initiation of Adults

Fifth Week of Lent

Psalm 22:16

M Y throat is dried up like baked clay, my tongue cleaves to my jaws; to the dust of death you have brought me down.

Q UARTADECIMA die ad vesperum Pascha Domini est: et in quintadecima solemnitatem celebrabitis altissimo Domino.

Fourteen days from now the Pasch of the Lord will begin, and on the fifteenth you will celebrate the great solemnity in honor of God Most High.

Monastic liturgy

DURING Lent it is considered important to avoid distractions and dissipations, and to ensure a certain concentration of effort on religious duties. Not only should worldly festivities be discontinued, but from the fifth and sixth centuries onwards we find that even feasts of the saints were eliminated or postponed to times outside the season of Lent. That explains why the present calendar of the universal church, from the middle of February onwards, gives us an unusual number of days on which there fall no feasts of the saints. In later times the veiling of pictures and statues during Lent was probably explained on similar grounds.

To limit the veiling of cross, statues and pictures to the last two weeks of Lent is a practice that came in only during the seventeenth century. The origin of this usage lies in the Fasting Veil ("Hungercloth") that was hung up in front of the altar at the beginning of Lent; we have evidence for it ever since the tenth century. The statues, after all, show the saints in their heavenly glory, and the crucifix of that period represented Christ as the triumphant king. The inclusion of the whole people in the discipline of public penance was also a factor tending to promote the custom. Just as public penitents were formerly excluded from the church, so now the whole people, being joined to them in spirit, should at least be shut out from the sight of the altar.   Josef Jungmann

THEY picked up stones to throw at him, but Jesus hid himself and went out of the temple.   John 8:59

YOU, neighbor God, if sometimes in the night
   I rouse you with loud knocking, I do so
only because I seldom hear you breathe;
I know: you are alone.
And should you need a drink, no one is there
to reach it to you, groping in the dark.
Always I hearken. Give but a small sign.
I am quite near.

Between us there is but a narrow wall,
and by sheer chance; for it would take
merely a call from your lips or from mine
to break it down,
and that without a sound.

The wall is built of your images.

They stand before you hiding you like names,
and when the light within me blazes high
that in my inmost soul I know you by,
the radiance is squandered on their frames.

And then my senses, which too soon grow lame,
Rainer Maria Rilke   exiled from you, must go their homeless ways.

FOR a brief moment I abandoned you,
   but with great compassion I will gather you.
In overflowing wrath for a moment
      I hid my face from you,
but with everlasting love I will have compassion on you,
Isaiah 54:7–8   says the LORD, your Redeemer.

O sun, whom light nor flight can match,
   Suppose thy lightful flightful wings
      Thou lend to me,
      And I could flee
   So far as thee the evening brings,
Even led to west he would me catch,
   Nor should I lurk with western things.

Do thou thy best, O secret night,
   In sable veil to cover me,
      Thy sable veil
      Shall vainly fail;
   With day unmasked my night shall be;
For night is day, and darkness light,
   O Father of all lights, to thee.

Mary Herbert
Seventeenth century

I look at the hills, and wonder
   From where will my help come?
My help comes from the Lord,
   The maker of earth and sky.
May God not let you stumble;
   May God your protector not sleep!
Truly God never rests or sleeps,
   Protecting Israel.
The Lord is your protector,
   The shade at your right hand.
The sun will not strike you by day,
   Nor the moon at night.
The Lord protects you from every evil;
   God protects your life.
The Lord will protect you, coming and going,
   Now, and forevermore.

Psalm 121

WITHOUT the sense of God's will we narrow down our lives to the material world. We are like misers crouching over their hoards and never seeing the skies; indeed we may narrow our prison still further, seeing in everything only the image of ourselves.

But once we are made aware of the greatness of events as expressions of God's love, once we see and live their sacramental value, then we are liberated into a greater life; the winds of eternity blow about us, and the infinite skies are our home, and we too walk the eternal hills.

Gerald Vann

I have no wit, no words, no tears;
My heart within me like a stone
Is numbed too much for hopes or fears;
    Look right, look left, I dwell alone;
I lift mine eyes, but dimmed with grief
    No everlasting hills I see;
My life is in the falling leaf:
    O Jesus, quicken me.

My life is like a faded leaf,
    My harvest dwindles to a husk;
Truly my life is void and brief
    And tedious in the barren dusk;
My life is like a frozen thing,
    No bud nor greenness can I see:
Yet rise it shall—the sap of Spring;
    O Jesus, rise in me.

Christina Georgina Rossetti
Nineteenth century

THE same leaves over and over again!
  They fall from giving shade above
To make one texture of faded brown
And fit the earth like a leather glove.
Before the leaves can mount again
To fill the trees with another shade,
They must go down past things coming up.
They must go down into the dark decayed.
They must be pierced by flowers and put
Beneath the feet of dancing flowers.
However it is in some other world,
I know that this is the way in ours.

Robert Frost

NOW green the larch; the hedges green,
  And early jonquils go a-begging.
The thoughtful man repairs his screen,
  The child emerges from his legging.

By daylight now, commuters come
  Homeward. The grackle, unimpeded,
Forsakes his charitable crumb
  To loot the lawn that's newly seeded.

Tulips are mocked for their display
  By periwinkles' self-effacement,
And benedicts on ladders sway,
  Fetching the storm sash to the basement.

Still slumbers the lethargic bee,
  The rosebush keeps its winter tag on,
But hatless to the A&P
  The shopper rides in station wagon.

Once more Good Humor's wheedling bell
  Brings out the spendthrift in the miser,
And everywhere's the lovely smell
  Of showers and soil and fertilizer.

Phyllis McGinley

'TIS night, and the landscape is lovely no more;
   For morn is approaching your charms to restore,
Nor yet for the ravage of winter I mourn,
But when shall spring visit the mouldering urn?

I mourn, but, ye woodlands, I mourn not for you;
Perfum'd with fresh fragrance and glitt'ring with dew:
Kind nature the embryo blossoms shall save,
Oh, when shall it dawn on the night of the grave?

*Early American
folk hymn*

THE human race may be compared to spikes of wheat in a
   field, rising, as it were, from the earth, awaiting their full
growth and development, and then in time being cut down by
the reaper, which is death.

*Cyril of Alexandria
Fifth century*

THE hour has come for the Son of Man to be glorified. Very
   truly, I tell you, unless a grain of wheat falls into the earth
and dies, it remains just a single grain; but if it dies, it bears
much fruit. Those who love their life lose it, and those who
hate their life in this world will keep it for eternal life. Whoever
serves me must follow me, and where I am, there will my
servant be also.

John 12:23–26

BEFORE the fruit is ripened by the sun,
   Before the petals or the leaves uncoil,
Before the first fine silken root is spun,
A seed is dropped and buried in the soil.

Before we gain the grace that comes through loss,
Before we live by more than bread and breath,
Before we lift in joy an empty cross,
We face with Christ the seed's renewing death.

Thomas H. Troeger

To each one of us Christ is saying: If you want your life and mission to be fruitful like mine, do as I. Be converted into a seed that lets itself be buried. Let yourself be killed. Do not be afraid. Those who shun suffering will remain alone. No one is more alone than the selfish. But if you give your life out of love for others, as I give mine for all, you will reap a great harvest.

Oscar Arnulfo Romero

PERISH the sword,
Perish the angry judgment,
Perish the bombs and hunger,
Perish the fight for gain;

Hallow our love,
Hallow the deaths of martyrs,
Hallow their holy freedom,
Hallowed be your name.

Frances W. Davis

WE shall not always plant while others reap
The golden increment of bursting fruit,
Not always countenance, abject and mute,
That lesser men should hold their brothers cheap;
Not everlasting while others sleep
Shall we beguile their limbs with mellow flute,
Not always bend to some more subtle brute;
We were not made eternally to weep.

The night whose sable breast relieves the stark,
White stars is no less lovely being dark,
And there are buds that cannot bloom at all
In light, but crumple, piteous, and fall;
So in the dark we hide the heart that bleeds,
And wait, and tend our agonizing seeds.

Countée Cullen

T HERE shall be a sowing of peace; the vine shall yield its
fruit, the ground shall give its produce, and the skies shall
Zechariah 8:12   give their dew.

T O you, O Lord, we cry and pray;
bless this sprouting seed,
strengthen it in the gentle movement of soft winds,
refresh it with the dew of heaven,
and let it grow to full maturity
Rituale Romanum   for the good of body and soul.

W E plough the fields and scatter
The good seed on the land,
But it is fed and watered
By God's almighty hand;
God sends the snow in winter,
The warmth to swell the grain,
The breezes and the sunshine,
And soft refreshing rain:

All good gifts around us,
Are sent from heav'n above,
M. Claudius   Then thank the Lord, O thank the Lord
Eighteenth century   For such great love.

J UST as the weeds are collected and burned up with fire at the
harvest, so will it be at the end of the age. The Son of Man
will send his angels, and they will collect out of his kingdom
all causes of sin and all evildoers, and they will throw them
into the furnace of fire, where there will be weeping and
gnashing of teeth. Then the righteous will shine like the sun in
Matthew 13:40–43   the kingdom of their Father. Let anyone with ears listen!

H EAR, O Father,
the cry of your Son,
who, to establish the new and everlasting covenant,
became obedient even unto death upon the cross.

Grant that, through all the trials of this life,
we may come to share more intimately
      in his redeeming passion
and so obtain the fruitfulness of the seed
      that falls to the earth and dies,
to be gathered as your harvest for the kingdom of heaven.   Italian sacramentary

I rock with grief, and am troubled at the voice of the enemy
and the clamor of the wicked.   Psalm 55:3–4

W HO rises up for me against the wicked?
Who stands up for me against evildoers?
If the Lord had not been my help,
      my soul would have soon lived in the land of silence.
The wicked band together against the life of the righteous,
      and condemn the innocent to death.   Psalm 94:16–17, 21

N ICODEMUS, who had gone to Jesus before, and who was
one of the Pharisees, asked, "Our law does not judge
people without first giving them a hearing to find out what
they are doing, does it?"   John 7:50–51

S USANNA would go into her husband's garden to walk. Every day two elders used to see her, going in and walking about, and they began to lust for her. They suppressed their consciences and turned away their eyes from looking to Heaven or remembering their duty to administer justice. Both were overwhelmed with passion for her, but they did not tell each other of their distress, for they were ashamed to disclose their lustful desire to seduce her. Day after day they watched eagerly to see her.

One day they said to each other, "Let us go home, for it is time for lunch." So they both left and parted from each other. But turning back, they met again; and when each pressed the other for the reason, they confessed their lust. Then together they arranged for a time when they could find her alone.

Once, while they were watching for an opportune day, she went in as before with only two maids, and wished to bathe in the garden, for it was a hot day. No one was there except the two elders, who had hidden themselves and were watching her. She said to her maids, "Bring me olive oil and ointments, and shut the garden doors so that I can bathe." They did as she told them: they shut the doors of the garden and went out by the side doors to bring what they had been commanded; they did not see the elders, because they were hiding.

When the maids had gone out, the two elders got up and ran to her. They said, "Look, the garden doors are shut, and no one can see us. We are burning with desire for you; so give your consent, and lie with us. If you refuse, we will testify against you that a young man was with you, and this was why you sent your maids away."

Susanna groaned and said, "I am completely trapped. For if I do this, it will mean death for me; if I do not, I cannot escape your hands. I choose not to do it; I will fall into your hands, rather than sin in the sight of the Lord."

Then Susanna cried out with a loud voice, and the two elders shouted against her. And one of them ran and opened the garden doors. When the people in the house heard the shouting in the garden, they rushed in at the side door to see what had happened to her. And when the elders told their story, the servants felt very much ashamed, for nothing like this had ever been said about Susanna.

The next day, when the people gathered at the house of her husband Joakim, the two elders came, full of their wicked plot to have Susanna put to death. In the presence of the people they said, "Send for Susanna daughter of Hilkiah, the wife of Joakim." So they sent for her. And she came with her parents, her children, and all her relatives.

Now Susanna was a woman of great refinement and beautiful in appearance. As she was veiled, the scoundrels ordered her to be unveiled, so that they might feast their eyes on her beauty. Those who were with her and all who saw her were weeping.

Then the two elders stood up before the people and laid their hands on her head. Through her tears she looked up toward Heaven, for her heart trusted in the Lord. The elders said, "While we were walking in the garden alone, this woman came in with two maids, shut the garden doors, and dismissed the maids. Then a young man, who was hiding there, came to her and lay with her. We were in a corner of the garden, and when we saw this wickedness we ran to them. Although we saw them embracing, we could not hold the man, because he was stronger than we, and he opened the doors and got away. We did, however, seize this woman and asked who the young man was, but she would not tell us. These things we testify."

Because they were elders of the people and judges, the assembly believed them and condemned her to death.

Then Susanna cried out with a loud voice, and said, "O eternal God, you know what is secret and are aware of all things before they come to be; you know that these men have given false evidence against me. And now I am to die, though I have done none of the wicked things that they have charged against me!"

The Lord heard her cry. Just as she was being led off to execution, God stirred up the holy spirit of a young lad named Daniel, and he shouted with a loud voice, "I want no part in shedding this woman's blood."

All the people turned to him and asked, "What is this you are saying?" Taking his stand among them he said, "Are you such fools, O Israelites, as to condemn a daughter of Israel without examination and without learning the facts? Return to court, for these men have given false evidence against her."

So all the people hurried back. And the rest of the elders said to him, "Come, sit among us and inform us, for God has given you the standing of an elder." Daniel said to them, "Separate them far from each other, and I will examine them."

When they were separated from each other, he summoned one of them and said to him, "You old relic of wicked days, your sins have now come home, which you have committed in the past, pronouncing unjust judgments, condemning the innocent and acquitting the guilty, though the Lord said, 'You shall not put an innocent and righteous person to death.' Now then, if you really saw this woman, tell me this: Under what tree did you see them being intimate with each other?" He answered, "Under a mastic tree." And Daniel said, "Very well! This lie has cost you your head, for the angel of God has received the sentence from God and will immediately cut you in two."

Then, putting him to one side, he ordered them to bring the other. And he said to him, "You offspring of Canaan and not of Judah, beauty has beguiled you and lust has perverted your heart. This is how you have been treating the daughters of Israel, and they were intimate with you through fear; but a daughter of Judah would not tolerate your wickedness. Now then, tell me: Under what tree did you catch them being intimate with each other?" He answered, "Under an ever-green oak." Daniel said to him, "Very well! This lie has cost you also your head, for the angel of God is waiting with the sword to split you in two, so as to destroy you both."

Daniel 13:7-60

Then the whole assembly raised a great shout and blessed God, who saves those who hope in the Lord.

O LORD my God, in you I take refuge;
    save me from all my pursuers, and deliver me,
or like a lion they will tear me apart;
    they will drag me away, with no one to rescue.

O LORD my God, if I have done this,
    if there is wrong in my hands,
if I have repaid my ally with harm
    or plundered my foe without cause,
then let the enemy pursue and overtake me,
    trample my life to the ground,
    and lay my soul in the dust.

Rise up, O LORD, in your anger;
    lift yourself up against the fury of my enemies;
    awake, O my God; you have appointed a judgment.
Let the assembly of the peoples be gathered around you,
    and over it take your seat on high.
The LORD judges the peoples;
    judge me, O LORD, according to my righteousness
    and according to the integrity that is in me.   Psalm 7:1–8

DANIEL the prophet, greatly beloved,
    when he saw the power of God, cried out:
"The court sat in judgment and the books were opened."
Consider well, O my soul.
Do you fast? Then despise not your brother and sister.
Do you abstain from food?
Then condemn not your neighbor,
    lest you burn as wax in the fire.
May Christ lead you without stumbling into his kingdom.   Byzantine Vespers

INSTEAD of asking fundamental questions—"What is fasting?" or "What is Lent?"—we satisfy ourselves with lenten symbolism. In church magazines and bulletins appear recipes for "delicious lenten dishes," and a parish might even raise some additional money by means of a well-advertised "tasty lenten dinner." So much in our churches is explained symbolically as interesting, colorful, and amusing customs and traditions, as something which connects us not so much with God and a new life in God but with the past and the customs of our ancestors, that it becomes increasingly difficult to discern behind this religious folklore the utter seriousness of religion. Let me stress that there is nothing wrong in the various customs themselves. When they appeared they were the means and the expressions of a society *taking religion seriously;* they were not symbols, but life itself. What happened, however, was that as life changed and became less and less shaped by religion in its totality, a few customs survived as symbols of a way of life no longer lived. And what survived was that which on the one hand is most colorful and on the other hand the least difficult. The spiritual danger here is that little by little one begins to understand religion itself as a system of symbols and customs rather than to understand the latter as a challenge to spiritual renewal and effort. More effort goes into preparing lenten dishes or Easter baskets than into fasting and participation in the spiritual reality of Easter. This means that as long as customs and traditions are not connected again with the total religious world view which produced them, as long as symbols are not taken *seriously,* the church will remain disconnected from life and have no power over life. Instead of symbolizing our "rich heritage," we must start integrating it into our real life.

Alexander Schmemann

I T is not some religious act which makes a Christian what he or she is, but participation in the suffering of God in the life of the world. This is *metanoia*. This being caught up into the messianic suffering of God in Jesus Christ takes a variety of forms in the New Testament. It appears in the call to disciple-ship, in Jesus' table fellowship with sinners, in conversions in the narrower sense of the word, in the act of the woman who was a sinner, an act which she performed without any specific confession of sin, in the healing of the sick, in Jesus' accep-tance of children. The centurion of Capernaum (who does not make any confession of sin) is held up by Jesus as a model of faith. There is nothing of religious asceticism here. The reli-gious act is always something *partial;* faith is always some-thing *whole,* an act involving the whole life. Jesus does not call us to a new religion but to a new life.   Dietrich Bonhoeffer

I knew I was a guilty woman. I felt like the ghost of myself just floating along in the draft from the stove to the sink and back again. I was not even afraid or unhappy. I was only surprised at myself and my devastations.   Joyce Cary

I NCLINAVIT se Jesus, scribebat in terra: Si quis sine peccato est, mittat in eam lapidem.

Nemo te condemnavit, mulier? Nemo, Domine. Nec ego te condemnado: jam amplius noli peccare.

Jesus bent down and wrote on the ground: If anyone is without sin, that one may stone her.

Woman, has no one condemned you? No one, Lord. Neither do I condemn you: From now on, do not sin.   Monastic liturgy

WOMAN

THOUGH I be worthy for my trespass
To suffer death abominable,
Yet, holy prophet, of your high grace,
In your judgment be merciable.

I will never more be so unstable:
O holy prophet, grant me mercy!
Of my sins unreasonable
With all my heart I am sorry.

JESUS

Where be thy foemen that did thee accuse?
Why have they left us two alone?

WOMAN

Because they could not themselves excuse,
With shame they fled hence every one.
But, gracious prophet, list to my moan:
Of my sorrow take compassion;
Now all mine enemies hence be gone,
Say me some word of consolation.

JESUS

For those sins that thou hast wrought
Hath any man condemned thee?

WOMAN

Nay, forsooth, that hath there nought;
But in your grace I put me.

JESUS

For me thou shalt not condemned be;
Go home again and walk at large:
Look that thou live in honesty,
And will no more to sin, I thee charge.

WOMAN
I thank you highly, holy prophet,
Of this great grace ye have me grant;
All my lewd life I shall down let,
And fond to be God's true servant.

JESUS
Now God, that died for humankind,
Save all these people both night and day;
And of our sins God us unbind,   Miracle play
High Lord of heaven, that best thou may.   Fifteenth century

A ND now she wept, after her long austerity, as though she
  would never be able to stop.   James Baldwin

L ET the sinner be punished, yes—but not by sinners. Let the
  law be carried out, but not by lawbreakers. This, unques-
tionably, is the voice of justice, justice that pierced those men
like a javelin. Looking into themselves, they realized their
guilt, and one by one they all went out. Two remained behind:
the miserable woman, and Mercy. The Lord raised his eyes,
and with a gentle look he asked her: "Has no one condemned
you?" She replied: "No one, sir." And he said: "Neither will I
condemn you."

What is this, Lord? Are you giving approval to immorality? Not
at all. Take note of what follows: "Go and sin no more." You
see then that the Lord does indeed pass sentence, but it is sin   Augustine of Hippo
he condemns, not people.   Fifth century

THE Christian tradition has often been accused of squeamishness about sex. The charge is a strange one, given Jesus' robustness with regard to sexual offenders. It should be noted that in his society, as in so many, women were the easy victims of the lusts of men. Of the latter he has no kind word to say. Indeed, one harsh one is recorded:

> You have heard the commandment, "You shall not commit adultery." What I say to you is: anyone who looks lustfully at a woman has already committed adultery with her in his thoughts."

He does not say "curiously" or "admiringly," not even "brazenly." He is not interested in the involuntary stirrings of passion that characterize all sexual attraction. Jesus goes to the heart of lust, which is desire. "With an eye to having her" might translate his words best. The helplessness of women before men who view them as possessions, ego-supports, or proofs of masculinity is what Jesus attacks. Woman the temptress he knows nothing about, though Jewish and Christian literature seems to find her on every page. The gospels tell only of Jesus' concern for woman had, woman used, woman rejected.

Gerard S. Sloyan

GIVE ear to my prayer, O God;
do not hide yourself from my supplication.
Attend to me, and answer me;
    I am troubled in my complaint.
I am distraught by the noise of the enemy,
    because of the clamor of the wicked.
For they bring trouble upon me,
    and in anger they cherish enmity against me.

My heart is in anguish within me,
  the terrors of death have fallen upon me.
Fear and trembling come upon me,
  and horror overwhelms me.
And I say, "O that I had wings like a dove!
  I would fly away and be at rest;
truly, I would flee far away;
  I would lodge in the wilderness."

It is not enemies who taunt me—
  I could bear that;
it is not adversaries who deal insolently with me—
  I could hide from them.
But it is you, my equal,
  my companion, my familiar friend,
  with whom I kept pleasant company.   Psalm 55:1–7, 12–14

THIS thought had lived in him with claws; or like a thirst he could never spit out, a repulsive need to get out of his system all that had happened—for whatever had happened had happened wrong; to clean it out of his self and bring it a little peace, a little order; to change the beginning, beginning with the past that always stupendously stank up till now—to change his life before the smell of it suffocated him.   Bernard Malamud

LORD, I confess my sin is great;
  Great is my sin. Oh! gently treat
With thy quick flower, thy momentary bloom;
  Whose life still pressing
  Is one undressing,
A steady aiming at a tomb.

George Herbert
Seventeenth century

ROUND about the mountain,
Round about the mountain,
My God's a-ruling,
And I shall rise in his arms.

You hypocrite, you concubine,
You placed among the swine,
You go to God with your lips and tongue,
But you leave your heart behind.

The Lord loves a sinner,
The Lord loves a sinner,
The Lord loves a sinner,
And I shall rise in his arms.

African-American
spiritual

TOO much searching conceals the thing we really ought to find. Nor is it certain that we have any urgent obligation to *find* sin in ourselves. How much sin is kept hidden from us by God, in mercy? After which God hides it even from God!

Thomas Merton

Psalm 102:5, 8

I forget to eat my bread. I am sleepless, and I moan. I am like a sparrow alone on the housetop.

AS on some lonely building top
The sparrow tells her moan,
Far from the tents of joy and hope
I sit and grieve alone.

Sense can afford no real joy
To souls that feel thy frown,
Lord, 'twas thy hand advanc'd me high;
Thy hand hath cast me down!

Early American
folk hymn

W HY is light given to one in misery,
and life to the bitter in soul,
who long for death, but it does not come,
    and dig for it more than for hidden treasures;
who rejoice exceedingly,
    and are glad when they find the grave?
Why is light given to one who cannot see the way,
    whom God has fenced in?
For my sighing comes like my bread,
    and my groanings are poured out like water.
Truly the thing that I fear comes upon me,
    and what I dread befalls me.
I am not at ease, nor am I quiet;
    I have no rest; but trouble comes.

Job 3:20–26

S OMETIMES I feel like a moanin' dove,
Sometimes I feel like a moanin' dove,
Sometimes I feel like a moanin' dove,
Wring my hands and cry, cry, cry!
Wring my hands and cry!

African-American
spiritual

Y OM KIPPUR, The Day of Atonement: Should we fast? The question is hotly debated. To fast would mean a surer, swifter death. We fasted here the whole year round. The whole year was Yom Kippur. But others said that we should fast simply because it was dangerous to do so. We should show God that even here, in this enclosed hell, we were capable of singing praises.

I did not fast, mainly to please my father, who had forbidden me to do so. But further, there was no longer any reason why I should fast. I no longer accepted God's silence. As I swallowed my bowl of soup, I saw in the gesture an act of rebellion and protest against God.

And I nibbled my crust of bread.

Elie Wiesel   In the depths of my heart, I felt a great void.

I would like to have bread,
such a lot of white bread.
Only for myself, all—
    fresh still, hot,
    fragrant with caraway—
with crackling crust
    brown, crunchy
bread.

And to sink my teeth into it and to fondle it in wonderment,
long to savor its taste all the way to the skies;
if I could even smell it, it would heal and soften
my insatiable stomach in its eternal hunger—

Ila and Henia Karmel   bread.

A FFLICTION makes God appear to be absent for a time, more absent than one dead, more absent than light in the utter darkness of a cell. A kind of horror submerges the whole soul. During this absence there is nothing to love. What is terrible is that if, in this darkness where there is nothing to love, the soul ceases to love, God's absence becomes final. The soul has to go on loving in the emptiness, or at least to go on wanting to love, though it may only be with an infinitesimal part of itself. Then, one day, God will come and be manifest to this soul and reveal the beauty of the world to it, as in the case of Job. But if the soul stops loving it falls, even in this life, into something almost equivalent to hell.   Simone Weil

I am not really frightened of anything, I feel so strong; it matters little whether you have to sleep on a hard floor, or whether you are only allowed to walk through certain specified streets, and so on—these are all minor vexations, so insignificant compared with the infinite riches and possibilities we carry within us.   Etty Hillesum

W E have this treasure in clay jars, so that it may be made clear that this extraordinary power belongs to God and does not come from us. We are afflicted in every way, but not crushed; perplexed, but not driven to despair; persecuted, but not forsaken; struck down, but not destroyed; always carrying in the body the death of Jesus, so that the life of Jesus may also be made visible in our bodies. For while we live, we are always being given up to death for Jesus' sake, so that the life of Jesus may be made visible in our mortal flesh.

2 Corinthians 4:7–11

I
F you invoke as Father the one who judges all people impartially according to their deeds, live in reverent fear during the time of your exile. You know that you were ransomed from the futile ways inherited from your ancestors, not with perishable things like silver or gold, but with the precious blood of Christ.

1 Peter 1:17–19

O
the beautiful treasure laid up for the wise,
How precious the value, how glorious the prize.
Far brighter than are diamonds on a prince's brow
And far richer than royalty can bestow.

Shaker hymn

W
HEN we are really honest with ourselves, we must admit that our lives are all that really belong to us. So it is how we use our lives that determines what kind of people we are.

César Chavez

O
BSERVE those who hold erroneous opinions concerning the grace of Jesus Christ, which has come to us, and see how they run counter to the mind of God! They concern themselves with neither works of charity, nor widows, nor orphans, nor the distressed, nor those in prison or out of it, nor the hungry or thirsty.

Ignatius of Antioch
Second century

I
T is in this darkness, when there is nothing left in us that can please or comfort our own minds, when we seem to be useless and worthy of all contempt, when we seem to have failed, when we seem to be destroyed and devoured, it is then that the deep and secret selfishness that is too close to us for us

to identify is stripped away from our souls. It is in this darkness that we find liberty. It is in this abandonment that we are made strong. This is the night which empties us and makes us pure.   Thomas Merton

THE moon shines bright, and the stars give a light:
   A little before it is day.
Our Lord, our God, now calls on us,
   And bids us awake and pray.

A human life is but a span
   And cut down in its flower;
We are here today, and tomorrow are gone,
   The creatures of an hour.   The Bellman's Song

DO not human beings have a hard service on earth,
   and are not their days like the days of a laborer?
Like a slave who longs for the shadow,
   and like laborers who look for their wages,
so I am allotted months of emptiness,
   and nights of misery are apportioned to me.
When I lie down I say, "When shall I rise?"
   But the night is long,
   and I am full of tossing until dawn.
My flesh is clothed with worms and dirt;
   my skin hardens, then breaks out again.
My days are swifter than a weaver's shuttle,
   and come to their end without hope.   Job 7:1–6

HUMILIATE capita vestra Deo.

Bow your heads to God.

Prayer over the people
Roman rite

Anthony Bloom

HUMILITY comes from the Latin word *humus,* fertile ground. The fertile ground is there, unnoticed, taken for granted, always there to be trodden upon. It is silent, inconspicuous, dark, and yet it is always ready to receive any seed, ready to give it substance and life. The more lowly, the more fruitful, because it becomes really fertile when it accepts all the refuse of the earth. It is so low that nothing can soil it, abase it, humiliate it; it has accepted the last place and cannot go any lower.

Rituale Romanum

WE humbly beg your clemency, O Lord, that you would render this soil fertile with rains in due season, that you would fill it with your blessing, and so grant that your people may be ever thankful for your gifts. Take infertility from the earth, and fill the hungry with your gifts, which the fruitful earth will yield in fullness, that the poor and needy may praise the name of your glory for ever and ever.

Robert Griffin

CHANGE and decay—in all around I see," we cheerfully sang in my days as a choirboy. Another stanza should have taught us this lesson: it is not only beauty and life that disappear in the cycle of time. Pain too passes, along with heartbreak, fear, and sickness. In a world doomed to fragility, death itself shall someday die.

CHRIST, the life of all the living,
Christ, the death of death, our foe,
Christ, yourself for me once giving
To the darkest depths of woe:
Through your suff'ring, death, and merit
Life eternal I inherit.
Ernst C. Homburg   Thousand, thousand thanks are due,
Seventeenth century   Dearest Jesus, unto you.

THE elders of daughter Zion
    sit on the ground in silence;
they have thrown dust on their heads
    and put on sackcloth;
the young girls of Jerusalem
    have bowed their heads to the ground.

My eyes are spent with weeping,
    my stomach churns;
my bile is poured out on the ground
    because of the destruction of my people,
because infants and babes faint
    in the streets of the city.

They cry to their mothers,
    "Where is bread and wine?"
as they faint like the wounded
    in the streets of the city,
as their life is poured out
    on their mothers' bosom.

What can I say for you, to what compare you,
    O daughter Jerusalem?
To what can I liken you, that I may comfort you,
    O virgin daughter Zion?
For vast as the sea is your ruin;
    who can heal you?   Lamentations 2:10–13

I late estrang'd—from Jesus wand'red,
    And thought each dang'rous poison good;
    But he in mercy long pursu'd me,
With cries of his redeeming blood.
    Though like Bartim'ous I was blinded
In nature's darkest light conceal'd,
    But Jesus' love remov'd my blindness,
And he his pard'ning grace reveal'd.   Early American hymn

O you who know us through and through,
   we languish in our wickedness,
   for sin has drugged our hearts.
In your love for humankind, O Lord,
heal our wounds and save us.

Byzantine prayer

WHEN the doctor cut off my son's cast the
   high scream of the saw filled the room
and Gabey's lap was covered with fluff like the
chaff of a new thing emerging, the
down in the hen-yard. Down the seam that
runs along the outside of the arm and
up the seam along the inside—that
line where the color of a white boy's arm
changes like a fish from belly-white to prismatic,
the saw ranged freely—the saw that does not cut flesh,
the doctor told us, smiling. Then the
horrible shriek ran down in a moment to nothing
and he took a sharp silver wedge like a
can-opener and jimmied at the cracks
until with a creak the glossy white
false arm cracked and there lay Gabey's
sweet dirty forearm, thin as a darkened twig.
He lifted it in astonishment, like a gift,
It's so light! he cried, a lot of light coming out of his eyes,
he fingered it and grinned, he picked up the
halves and put them together and gripped it and
carried it out through the waiting room and
everyone smiled the way you smile at a wedding, so
deep in us the desire to be healed and joined.

Sharon Olds

LET our days of fasting please you, Lord, and so may they
   erase the memory of our sins, make us worthy of your
favor and bring us on to a healing that lasts forever.

Missal of Pius V

H AD not the Lord been with us, let Israel say, had not the Lord been with us!

Psalm 124:1

M Y child, when you come to serve the Lord,
prepare yourself for testing.
Accept whatever befalls you,
    and in times of humiliation be patient.
For gold is tested in the fire,
    and those found acceptable,
    in the furnace of humiliation.

Sirach 2:1, 4–5

S HADRACH, Meshach, and Abednego answered the king, "O Nebuchadnezzar, we have no need to present a defense to you in this matter. If our God whom we serve is able to deliver us from the furnace of blazing fire and out of your hand, O king, let God deliver us. But if not, be it known to you, O king, that we will not serve your gods and we will not worship the golden statue that you have set up."

Then Nebuchadnezzer was so filled with rage against Shadrach, Meshach, and Abednego that his face was distorted. He ordered the furnace heated up seven times more than was customary, and ordered some of the strongest guards in his army to bind Shadrach, Meshach, and Abednego and to throw them into the furnace of blazing fire. So the men were bound, still wearing their tunics, their trousers, their hats, and their other garments, and they were thrown into the furnace of blazing fire.

Daniel 3:16–21

WHEN the layers of gas had covered everything, there was silence in the dark sky of the room for perhaps a minute, broken only by shrill, racking coughs and the gasps of those too far gone in their agonies to offer a devotion. And first a stream, then a cascade, an irrepressible, majestic torrent, the poem that through the smoke of fires and above the funeral pyres of history the Jews—who for two thousand years did not bear arms and who never had either missionary empires nor colored slaves—the old love poem that they traced in letters of blood on the earth's hard crust unfurled in the gas chamber, enveloped it, vanquished its somber, abysmal snickering: *"Shema Yisrael Adonoi Elohenu Adonoi Eh'oth . . .* Hear, O Israel, the Lord is our God, the Lord is One. O Lord, by your grace you nourish the living, and by your great pity you resurrect the dead, and you uphold the weak, cure the sick, break the chains of slaves. And faithfully you keep your promises to those who sleep in the dust. Who is like unto you, O merciful Father, and who could be like unto you . . . ?"

The voices died one by one in the course of the unfinished poem. The dying children had already dug their nails into Ernie's thighs, and Golda's embrace was already weaker, her kisses were blurred when, clinging fiercely to her beloved's neck, she exhaled a harsh sigh: "Then I'll never see you again? Never again?"

Ernie managed to spit up the needle of fire jabbing at his throat, and as the woman's body slumped against him, its eyes wide in the opaque night, he shouted against the unconscious Golda's ear, "In a little while, *I swear it!*" And then he knew that he could do nothing more for anyone in the world, and in the flash that preceded his own annihilation he remembered, happily, the legend of Rabbi Chanina ben Teradion, as Mordecai had joyfully recited it: "When the gentle rabbi, wrapped in the scrolls of the Torah, was flung upon the pyre by the Romans for having taught the Law, and when they lit the fagots, the branches still green to make his torture last, his pupils said, 'Master, what do you see?' And Rabbi Chanina answered, 'I see the parchment burning, but the letters are taking wing,'" . . . *"Ah, yes, surely, the letters are taking wing,"* Ernie repeated as the flame blazing in his chest rose suddenly to his head. With dying arms he embraced Golda's body in an already unconscious gesture of loving protection, and they were found that way half an hour later by the team of *Sonder-kommando* responsible for burning the Jews in the crematory ovens. And so it was for millions, who turned from *Luft-menschen* into *Luft.* I shall not translate. So this story will not finish with some tomb to be visited *in memoriam.*

For the smoke that rises from crematoriums obeys physical laws like any other: the particles come together and disperse according to the wind that propels them. The only pilgrimage, estimable reader, would be to look with sadness at a stormy sky now and then.

André Schwarz-Bart

B E merciful to me, O God, be merciful to me,
for in you my soul takes refuge;
in the shadow of your wings I will take refuge,
    until the destroying storms pass by.

My heart is steadfast, O God,
    my heart is steadfast.
I will sing and make melody.
    Awake, my soul!
Awake, O harp and lyre!
I will awaken the dawn.

I will give thanks to you, O Lord, among the peoples;
    I will sing praises to you among the nations.
For your steadfast love is as high as the heavens;
    your faithfulness extends to the clouds.   Psalm 57:1, 7–10

O sages standing in God's holy fire
    As in the gold mosaic of a wall,
Come from the holy fire, perne in a gyre,
And be the singing-masters of my soul.
Consume my heart away; sick with desire
And fastened to a dying animal
It knows not what it is; and gather me
Into the artifice of eternity.   William Butler Yeats

L ORD, enfold me in the depths of your heart; and there hold me, refine, purge, and set me on fire, raise me aloft, until my own self knows utter annihilation.

Teilhard de Chardin

C OME, my Light, and illumine my darkness.
Come, my Life, and revive me from death.
Come, my Physician, and heal my wounds.
Come, Flame of divine love,
    and burn up the thorns of my sins,
kindling my heart with the flame of thy love.

Dimitrii of Rostov
Seventeenth century

O NE who breaks an unjust law must do so openly, lovingly, and with a willingness to accept the penalty. I submit that an individual who breaks a law that conscience tells him is unjust, and who willingly accepts the penalty of imprisonment in order to arouse the conscience of the community over its injustice, is in reality expressing the highest respect for law.

Of course, there is nothing new about this kind of civil disobedience. It was evidenced sublimely in the refusal of Shadrach, Meshach, and Abednego to obey the laws of Nebuchadnezzar, on the ground that a higher moral law was at stake.

Martin Luther King, Jr.

K ING Nebuchadnezzar was astonished and rose up quickly. He said to his counselors, "Was it not three men that we threw bound into the fire?" They answered the king, "True, O king." He replied, "But I see four men unbound, walking in the middle of the fire, and they are not hurt; and the fourth has the appearance of a god." Nebuchadnezzar then approached the door of the furnace of blazing fire and said, "Shadrach, Meshach, and Abednego, servants of the Most High God, come out!"

Daniel 3:24–26

H EBREW children in the fiery furnace.
And they begin to pray,
And the good Lord smote that fire out.
Oh, wasn't that a mighty day?
Good Lord, wasn't that a mighty day?
   Climbin' up the mountain, children.
      Didn't come here for to stay,
   If I nevermore see you again,
      Gonna meet you at the judgment day.

African-American
spiritual

W ONDERFUL to come out living
From the fiery furnace-blast,
But yet more, that after testing
   I shall be fine gold at last;
Time of cleansing! Time of winnowing!
   Yet 'tis calm, without dismay;
One who soon shall be my refuge
   Holds the winnowing-fan today.

Ann Griffiths
Eighteenth century

O God, you subdued the flames of fire for the three
youths. Mercifully grant that we your servants may not
be consumed by the flames of immorality.

Missal of Pius V

N O one can lay any foundation other than the one that has been laid; that foundation is Jesus Christ. Now if anyone builds on the foundation with gold, silver, precious stones, wood, hay, straw—the work of each builder will become visible, for the Day will disclose it, because it will be revealed with fire, and the fire will test what sort of work each has done.

1 Corinthians 3:11–13

B LESS our God, O peoples,
let the sound of God's praise be heard,
who has kept us among the living,
    and has not let our feet slip.
For you, O God, have tested us;
    you have tried us as silver is tried.
You brought us into the net;
    you laid burdens on our backs;
you let people ride over our heads;
    we went through fire and through water;
yet you have brought us out to a spacious place.

Psalm 66:8–12

W HEN Polycarp had wafted up the *Amen* and finished the prayer, the men attending to the fire lit it; and when a mighty flame shot up, we, who were privileged to see it, saw a wonderful thing; and we have been spared to tell the tale to the rest. The fire produced the likeness of a vaulted chamber, like a ship's sail bellying to the breeze, and surrounded the martyr's body as with a wall; and he was in the center of it, not as burning flesh, but as bread that is baking, or as gold and silver refined in a furnace! In fact, we even caught an aroma such as the scent of incense or of some other precious spice.

The Martyrdom
of Polycarp
Second century

WHAT is that coming up from the wilderness,
like a column of smoke,
perfumed with myrrh and frankincense,
    with all the fragrant powders of the merchant?
Look, it is the litter of Solomon!   Song of Songs 3:6–7

MAY my song rise like incense in thy presence. And for us
may it be a perfume of consolation, of goodness and
grace, so that these fumes will drive out every phantom from
the mind and body, leaving us, as the Apostle Paul phrased it,
smelling sweetly of God. May all the attacks of demons fly
from this incense, like dust before the wind, like smoke before
the dancing flames.

Anglo-Saxon blessing
of incense

THE meaning of incense used at a grave can be best
understood from the old prayer spoken as the coffin was
incensed after it had been placed in the ground: "May God—
Father, the Son, and Holy Spirit—delight your soul with heavenly fragrance." In this symbolic language heaven was seen as
a great house of God that is filled with the fragrance of incense
(and of what can the words "house of God" be more fittingly
used than of heaven?); the wishes and prayers of relatives and
friends at the grave were that the dead person might dwell
forever in this house of God where all is adoration.

If it be true that incense is a sign of adoration, then it must
continue to be used in an age of increasing awareness that
adoration is the breath of life.   Balthasar Fischer

THAT, then, is the evening sacrifice: the Lord's own passion, his cross, the offering on it of the saving victim, of that holocaust which is acceptable to God. And by his rising, Christ turned that evening sacrifice into a morning oblation.

Similarly, the pure prayer which ascends from a faithful heart will be like incense rising from a hallowed altar. No fragrance can be more pleasing to God than that of the Son. May all the faithful breathe out the same perfume.

Augustine of Hippo
Fifth century

Hebrews 5:7

IN the days when he was in the flesh, Christ offered prayers and supplications with loud cries and tears to the one who was able to save him from death, and he was heard because of his reverence.

JERUSALEM sinned grievously,
  so she has become a mockery;
all who honored her despise her,
    for they have seen her nakedness;
she herself groans,
    and turns her face away.

Her uncleanness was in her skirts;
    she took no thought of her future;
her downfall was appalling,
    with none to comfort her.
"O LORD, look at my affliction,
    for the enemy has triumphed!"

All her people groan
  as they search for bread;
they trade their treasures for food
  to revive their strength.
Look, O LORD, and see
  how worthless I have become.

Is it nothing to you, all you who pass by?
  Look and see
if there is any sorrow like my sorrow.

Lamentations 1:8–9,
11–12

L ORD, you have been our dwelling place
  in all generations.
Before the mountains were brought forth,
  or ever you had formed the earth and the world,
  from everlasting to everlasting you are God.

You turn us back to dust,
  and say, "Turn back, you mortals."
For a thousand years in your sight
  are like yesterday when it is past,
  or like a watch in the night.

You sweep them away; they are like a dream,
  like grass that is renewed in the morning;
in the morning it flourishes and is renewed;
  in the evening it fades and withers.

Psalm 90:1–6

IF God has any voice it is the wind.
It is death made loud:
nowhereness bellowing,
now reedy along the copper eaves,
now ballooned to a manifold softness by a tree,
now scraping like flint on the surface of water,
making arrowhead wrinkles,
seeking somewhere to stop and be.

I lie here listening.
God is crying, *for-*
giiiive, demanding, *fore-*
go-ooo, proclaiming, *no-*
wheerrre, and begging,

John Updike   *let go-oo-ohhh.*

THE world said, "Love cuts like the cold wind, and the will
of God is plain as the winter. Where is the summer will of
God? Where are the green seasons of God's will? Where is the
Flannery O'Connor   spring and summer of God's will?"

LOVE is not a cultural nicety; it does not ratify one's desire;
nor does it make one fit in or feel good. Love is God's self-
communication through Jesus, the Word made flesh; and in
human affairs, love is the absolute will that calls forth each
person to God. Love reveals the individual's duty that furthers
the divine plan for all creation. This "winter will," plain and
perennially out of season to tepid human expectation, cuts
Richard Giannone   and burns to prepare for the glory to come.

WHEN the fast makes its appearance, like a kind of spiritual springtime, let us as soldiers burnish our weapons, and as harvesters sharpen our sickles, and as sailors order our thoughts against the waves of extravagant desires, and as travelers set out on the journey toward heaven, and as wrestlers strip for the contest. For the believer is at once a harvester, a sailor, a soldier, a wrestler and a traveler.

John Chrysostom
Fourth century

THE snares of death encompassed me;
the pangs of Sheol laid hold on me;
I suffered distress and anguish.
Then I called on the name of the LORD:
"O LORD, I pray, save my life!"

Gracious is the LORD, and righteous;
our God is merciful.
The LORD protects the simple;
when I was brought low, God saved me.
Return, O my soul, to your rest,
for the LORD has dealt bountifully with you.

For you have delivered my soul from death,
my eyes from tears,
my feet from stumbling.
I walk before the LORD
in the land of the living.
I kept my faith, even when I said,
"I am greatly afflicted."

Psalm 116:3–10

THOSE struck down by affliction are at the foot of the cross, almost at the greatest possible distance from God. It must not be thought that sin is a greater distance. Sin is not a distance, it is a turning of our gaze in the wrong direction.

Simone Weil

O mortal one, remember well,
When Christ our Lord was born,
He was crucified between two thieves,
And crowned with the thorn,
And crowned with the thorn.

O mortal one, remember well,
When Christ died on the rood,
'Twas for our sins and wicked ways
Christ shed his precious blood,
Christ shed his precious blood.

O mortal one, remember well,
When Christ was wrapped in clay,
He was taken to a sepulchre
Where no one ever lay,
Where no one ever lay.

English carol
Nineteenth century

THE people who hanged Christ never, to do them justice, accused him of being a bore—on the contrary; they thought him too dynamic to be safe. It has been left for later generations to muffle up that shattering personality and surround him with an atmosphere of tedium. We have very efficiently pared the claws of the Lion of Judah, certified him "meek and mild," and recommended him as a fitting household pet for pale curates and pious old ladies. To those who knew him, however, he in no way suggested a milk-and-water person; they objected to him as a dangerous firebrand. True, he was tender to the unfortunate, patient with honest inquirers, and humble before heaven; but he insulted respectable clergymen by calling them hypocrites; he referred to King Herod as "that fox"; he went to parties in disreputable company and was looked upon as a "gluttonous man and a wine-bibber, a friend of publicans and sinners"; he assaulted indignant tradesmen and threw them and their belongings out of the Temple; he drove a coach-and-horses through a number of sacrosanct and hoary regulations; he cured diseases by any means that came handy, with a shocking casualness in the matter of other people's pigs and property; he showed no proper deference for wealth or social position; when confronted with neat dialectical traps, he displayed a paradoxical humour that affronted serious-minded people, and he retorted by asking disagreeably searching questions that could not be answered by rule of thumb. He was emphatically not a dull man in his human lifetime, and if he was God, there can be nothing dull about God either. But he had "a daily beauty in his life that made us ugly," and officialdom felt that the established order of things would be more secure without him. So they did away with God in the name of peace and quietness.   Dorothy Sayers

H E is the lonely greatness of the world—
(His eyes are dim)
His power it is holds up the Cross
    That holds up him.

He takes the sorrow of the threefold hour—
    (His eyelids close)
Round him and round, the wind—his Spirit—where
    It listeth blows.

And so the wounded greatness of the world
    In silence lies—
And death is shattered by the light from out
    Those darkened eyes.   Madeleine Caron Rock

A LMIGHTY God, restore the dignity of our human condition, long disfigured by excess but now renewed by the
discipline of self-denial.   Missal of Pius V

THERE are countless prophets of sacred causes that espouse the rights of the poor. Some are known; the vast majority are anonymous. They all share the impotence and helplessness of Jesus on the cross. They are asked to accept the most difficult assignment: to hope against hope, to love what does not seem to be present to them, and to believe in what they cannot see. They are asked to endure the worst plight a human being can experience: to die feeling abandoned by the God for whom they lived and sacrificed their lives.

Still, they do not abandon God. They surrender themselves to God in complete confidence. In total inner emptiness they cling to the nameless mystery that is infinitely beyond them. For this mysterious God holds the secret meaning of all their failed quests, of all the absurdities of history. To die like that is to share Jesus' death on the cross. It is to share his redeeming mystery, which will go on through history until the world reaches its end and fulfillment in the liberation of the last Leonardo Boff   sinner who opens to God's mercifulness.

WHEN all is said and done, what the world most needs from the church is not so much instruction about the nature of the mystery as a glimpse of the mystery itself operative in us. It already knows its own passion, and the vastness of the shipwreck of history; it waits for us to show it the power of Christ's passion and to lift our agony into his.

Adam and Jesus, you see—history's agent and history's Lord— have been in the same room all along. What a pity we have so Robert Farrar Capon   often failed to introduce them.

I say that we should visit Christ while there is opportunity, take care of him and feed him. We should clothe Christ and welcome him. We should honor him, not only at our table, like some; not only with ointments, like Mary; not only with a sepulchre, like Joseph of Arimathea; nor with things which have to do with his burial, like Nicodemus, who loved Christ only by half; nor finally with gold, incense and myrrh, like the Magi, who came before all those whom we have mentioned.

But, as the Lord of all desires mercy and not sacrifice, and as compassion is better than tens of thousands of fat rams, let us offer him this mercy through the needy and those who are at present cast down on the ground.

Gregory of Nazianzus
Fourth century

MORTAL, these bones are the whole house of Israel. They say, "Our bones are dried up, and our hope is lost; we are cut off completely." Therefore prophesy, and say to them, Thus says the LORD God: I am going to open your graves, and bring you up from your graves, O my people; and I will bring you back to the land of Israel. And you shall know that I am the LORD, when I open your graves, and bring you up from your graves, O my people. I will put my spirit within you, and you shall live, and I will place you on your own soil.

Ezekiel 37:11–14

THE Rabbis chose Ezekiel 37, the prophetic vision of resurrection, as the reading from the Prophets for the Shabbat of Passover. Of course, the Rabbis intended a dual message. The past Exodus points to a future redemption in which Israel will be restored to the land.

Irving Greenberg

I will let you find me, says the LORD, and I will restore your fortunes and gather you from all the nations and all the places where I have driven you, says the LORD, and I will bring you back to the place from which I sent you into exile.

Jeremiah 29:14

C OME, let us return to the LORD;
for it is he who has torn, and he will heal us;
he has struck down, and he will bind us up.
After two days he will revive us;
on the third day he will raise us up,

Hosea 6:1–2   that we may live before him.

T HE third day will begin in the new heaven and the new
earth when these bones, namely, the whole house of
Israel, will be raised up on the great day of the Lord after death
has been overcome. And so, the resurrection of Christ will
embrace the mystery of the resurrection of the whole body of
Christ. Just as that physical body of Christ was nailed to the
cross and buried and afterwards raised to life, so the whole
body of Christ's saints has been nailed to the cross with Christ
and now no longer lives. Just like Paul, they glory in nothing

Origen   other than the cross of our Lord Jesus Christ, by which they are
Third century   crucified to the world and the world to them.

A ND the Son of Man was not crucified once for all,
The blood of the Martyrs not shed once for all,
The lives of the Saints not given once for all:
But the Son of Man is crucified always,

T. S. Eliot   And there shall be Martyrs and Saints.

A LMIGHTY God, whose most dear Son went not up to joy
but first he suffered pain, and entered not into glory
before he was crucified: Mercifully grant that we, walking in
the way of the cross, may find it none other than the way of life
and peace; through the same thy Son Jesus Christ our Lord,

Book of   who liveth and reigneth with thee and the Holy Spirit, one
Common Prayer   God, for ever and ever.

I say to myself: I will speak in the Lord's name no more. But then it becomes like a fire burning in my heart, imprisoned in my bones.

Jeremiah 20:9

O tough and steely hearts! O hearts more hard than flint or other stone! O great unthankfulness that removes us so far away from God that it is a marvel above all marvels that God looks so far down upon such extreme ingratitude!

John Fisher
Sixteenth century

THE crucifixion of Jesus is not to be understood simply in good liberal fashion as the sacrifice of a noble man, nor should we too quickly assign a cultic, priestly theory of atonement to the event. Rather, we might see in the crucifixion of Jesus the ultimate act of prophetic criticism in which Jesus announces the end of a world of death (the same announcement as that of Jeremiah) and takes that death into his own person. Therefore we say that the ultimate criticism is that God embraces the death that people must die. The criticism consists not in standing over against but in standing with; the ultimate criticism is not one of triumphant indignation but one of passion and compassion that completely and irresistibly undermine the world of competence and competition. The contrast is stark and total: this *passionate* man set in the midst of *numbed* Jerusalem. And only the *passion* can finally penetrate the *numbness*.

Walter Brueggemann

I will pour out a spirit of compassion and supplication on the house of David and the inhabitants of Jerusalem, so that, when they look on the one whom they have pierced, they shall mourn for him, as one mourns for an only child, and weep bitterly over him, as one weeps over a firstborn.

Zechariah 12:10

LOOK, my soul, how God loves you,
See how for you God relents. But
Your spite torments God more than
The tortures of the executioner.

The Lord of the whole world stands
Before a judge. Out of great contempt
For the white garment with which he is adorned,
The silent lamb is mocked.

In exchange for my sins, his tormentors
Sorely scourge his back. Come sinners,
Behold what the torturers are preparing for you—
From the blood of Jesus, a fountain of living water
For the cold of heart.

Let worldly pride boast what it will.
In its temple it plaits from the rose
A wreath whose thorn wounds
The king, scarlet robed and mocked.

O cold soul, who is this for whom
You do not warm? My heart, who
Is this for whom you do not allow
Everything to melt? Out of fiery love
Your Jesus sheds his blood in abundance.

May my heart dissolve in tears,
For it has grossly offended you, my Jesus.
I am in anguish! How I am in anguish! for the
Burden of my spite—for the love of you, my Jesus.

The Bitter Lamentations

WHAT are human beings,
that you make so much of them,
that you set your mind on them,
visit them every morning,
test them every moment?

Will you not look away from me for a while,
    let me alone until I swallow my spittle?
If I sin, what do I do to you, you watcher of humanity?
    Why have you made me your target?
    Why have I become a burden to you?
Why do you not pardon my transgression
    and take away my iniquity?
For now I shall lie in the earth;
    you will seek me, but I shall not be.   Job 7:17–21

THIS mutilated flesh, our victim,
    Explains too nakedly, too well,
The spell of the asparagus garden,
    The aim of our chalk-pit game; stamps,
Birds' eggs are not the same, behind the wonder
    Of tow-paths and sunken lanes,
Behind the rapture on the spiral stair,
    We shall always now be aware
Of the deed into which they lead, under
    The mock chase and mock capture,
The racing and tussling and splashing,
    The panting and the laughter,
Be listening for the cry and stillness
    To follow after: wherever
The sun shines, brooks run, books are written,
    There will also be this death.   W. H. Auden

O earth, do not cover my blood;
    let my outcry find no resting place.   Job 16:18

THE paper said the man's name was Ronald Ferguson, 46, an ex-miner, no fixed abode. He drank methylated spirits and slept in bus shelters. There is an element of human wastage in all societies. But—in that house—it was believed that when we had changed the world (yes, in spite of, beyond the purges, the liquidations, the forced labor and imprisonments)—the "elimination of private conflicts set up by the competitive nature of capitalist society" would help people to live, even people like this one, who, although white and privileged under the law of the country, couldn't make a place for himself. I had seen my brother dead and my mother and father; each time the event itself, so close to me, was obscured from me by sorrow and explained by accident, illness, or imprisonment. It was *caused* by the chlorinated water with flecks of his pink breakfast bacon in it that I saw pumped from my brother's mouth when he was taken from the pool; by that paralysis that blotted out my mother limb by limb; by the fever that my father smelled of, dying for his beliefs in a prison hospital.

Nadine Gordimer   But this death was the mystery itself.

O LORD, you have enticed me,
  and I was enticed;
you have overpowered me,
  and you have prevailed.
I have become a laughingstock all day long;
  everyone mocks me.
For whenever I speak, I must cry out,
  I must shout, "Violence and destruction!"
For the word of the LORD has become for me
  a reproach and derision all day long.
If I say, "I will not mention him,
  or speak any more in his name,"
then within me there is something like a burning fire
  shut up in my bones;
I am weary with holding it in,
Jeremiah 20:7–9   and I cannot.

G OING to thy Passion that frees from passion all the posterity of Adam and Eve, thou hast said, O Christ, to thy friends: "I have desired to eat this Passover with you; for the Father has sent me to cleanse the world from sin."   Byzantine Matins

W E have to eat bitter herbs. These stand for the bitter sufferings we must undergo, and we should greatly value the endurance they demand. It would indeed be quite absurd if those desiring to serve God imagined they could achieve great virtue, and glory in the supreme reward, without having first contended for it and given proof of the most steadfast courage. The approach to this goal is rugged and steep, and it is inaccessible to most people. It becomes easy only for those whose desire to arrive is so strong that they are dismayed by nothing and are ready to face hardship and toil. Christ's own words urge us to do this. "Enter by the narrow gate, for the gate is wide and the road easy that leads to damnation, and those who enter by it are many. The gate is narrow and the road hard that leads to life, and those who find it are few."   Cyril of Alexandria
Fifth century

I regard everything as loss because of the surpassing value of knowing Christ Jesus my Lord. For his sake I have suffered the loss of all things, and I regard them as rubbish, in order that I may gain Christ and be found in him, not having a righteousness of my own that comes from the law, but one that comes through faith in Christ, the righteousness from God based on faith.

Not that I have already obtained this or have already reached the goal; but I press on to make it my own, because Christ Jesus has made me his own. Beloved, I do not consider that I have made it my own; but this one thing I do: forgetting what lies behind and straining forward to what lies ahead, I press on toward the goal for the prize of the heavenly call of God in Christ Jesus.   Philippians 3:8–9,
12–14

G OD of infinite wisdom,
we pray that these your servants,
who look forward to baptism,
may follow in the footsteps of Paul
and trust not in flesh and blood,
but in the call of your grace.

Probe their hearts and purify them,
so that, freed from all deception,
they may never look back
but strive always toward what is to come.

May they count everything as a loss
compared with the unsurpassed worth of knowing your Son
and so gain him as their eternal reward,
for he is Lord for ever and ever.

*Rite of Christian
Initiation of Adults*

T HOSE who receive strength from the Light and great power
and authority over their enemies are like well-trained
athletes, stripping to confront their opponents with courage
and confidence.

Gregory of Nyssa
Fourth century

A THLETES exercise self-control in all things; they do it to
receive a perishable wreath, but we an imperishable one.

1 Corinthians 9:25

T HE sight of a wounded boxer wearing a victor's crown
would make someone ignorant of the games think only of
the boxer's wounds and how painful they must be. Such a
person would know nothing of the happiness the crown gives.
And it is the same when people see the things we suffer
without knowing why we do so. It naturally seems to them to

be suffering pure and simple. They see us struggling and facing danger, but beyond their vision are the rewards, the crowns of victory—all we hope to gain through the contest!

John Chrysostom
Fourth century

T HIS is the day of jubilee,
God's going to build up Zion's walls,
The Lord has set the people free,
God's going to build up Zion's walls!

We want no cowards in our band,
God's going to build up Zion's walls,
We'll make a valiant-hearted stand,
God's going to build up Zion's walls!

Going to take my breastplate, sword and shield,
God's going to build up Zion's walls,
And march out boldly in the field,
God's going to build up Zion's walls!

Great day! Great day, the righteous marching!
Great day! God's going to build up Zion's walls!

African-American
spiritual

W E too, then, when we suffer anything for Christ's sake, should do so not only with courage, but even with joy. If we have to go hungry, let us be glad as if we were at a banquet. If we are insulted, let us be elated as though we had been showered with praises. If we lose all we possess, let us consider ourselves the gainers. If we provide for the poor, let us regard ourselves as the recipients. Anyone who does not give in this way will find it difficult to give at all. So when you wish to distribute alms, do not think only of what you are giving away; think rather of what you are gaining, for your gain will exceed your loss.

John Chrysostom
Fourth century

Missal of Pius V W E ask, almighty God, that those who discipline their bodies by fasting from food may fast also from sin and so seek your justice.

O God,
Giver of all spiritual growth and advance,
who by the power of the Holy Spirit
   strengthens in inconstant minds
   the beginnings of knowledge of the faith;
we implore you, O Lord, in your kindness
to send forth your blessing upon this oil.

Grant to those who are to come to the cleansing
   of spiritual rebirth
purification of mind and body
through anointing with this your creature.

If any defilement of hostile spirits remains in them,
may it depart at the touch of this holy oil,
and leave no place for wicked spirits,
no opportunity for the powers that have been put to flight,
no freedom for lurking evils.

For those who are coming to the faith
   and are about to be cleansed
      by the work of your Holy Spirit,
may this anointing that has been prepared
   be useful toward the salvation
      which they will obtain in the sacrament of baptism

Blessing of the oil
of catechumens by the birth of heavenly regeneration.

THEY shall come and sing aloud on the height of Zion,
  and they shall be radiant
    over the goodness of the LORD,
over the grain, the wine, and the oil,
    and over the young of the flock and the herd;
their life shall become like a watered garden,
    and they shall never languish again.   Jeremiah 31:12

IF you believe, you will see the glory of God.   John 11:40

EVEN the dead will bow down to the Lord,
  And those who are dust will kneel before God.
And when my life has come to an end,
    My offspring will serve the Lord.
Declare God's justice to future ages;
    Tell those yet unborn, what the Lord has done!   Psalm 22:29–31

LAZARUS amicus noster dormit: eamus, et a somno
  excitemus eum.

Our friend Lazarus has fallen asleep. Let us go now and we
shall wake him from his sleep.   Monastic liturgy

W HEN Mary came where Jesus was and saw him, she knelt at his feet and said to him, "Lord, if you had been here, my brother would not have died." When Jesus saw her weeping, and the Jews who came with her also weeping, he was greatly disturbed in spirit and deeply moved. He said, "Where have you laid him?" They said to him, "Lord, come and see." Jesus began to weep.

John 11:32–35

W HEN Jesus wept, a falling tear
in mercy flowed beyond all bound;
when Jesus groaned, a trembling fear
seized all the guilty world around.

William Billings
Eighteenth century

T HERE is grief work to be done in the present that the future may come. There is mourning to be done for those who do not know of the deathliness of their situation. There is mourning to be done with those who know pain and suffering and lack the power or freedom to bring it to speech. The saying is a harsh one, for it sets this grief work as the precondition of joy. It announces that those who have not cared enough to grieve will not know joy.

The mourning is a precondition in another way too. It is not a formal, external requirement but rather the only door and route to joy. Seen in that context, this is not just a neat saying but a summary of the entire theology of the cross. Only that kind of anguished disengagement permits fruitful yearning and only the public embrace of deathliness permits newness to come. We are at the edge of knowing this in our personal lives, for we understand a bit of the processes of grieving. But we have yet to learn and apply it to the reality of society. And finally, we have yet to learn it about God, who grieves in ways hidden from us and who waits to rejoice until God's promises are fully kept.

Walter Brueggemann

E TERNAL Father,
whose glory is the human person fully alive,
we see your compassion revealed in the tears of Jesus
     for Lazarus his friend.

Look today upon the distress of your church,
mourning and praying for her children
dead in their sins.
By the power of your Spirit call them back to life.   Italian sacramentary

O Christ, mystically thou hast shed tears over thy friend,
and hast raised from the dead Lazarus who lay without
life; and thou hast shown tender compassion for him in thy
love toward humankind. Learning of thy coming, O Savior, a
multitude of children went out bearing palms in their hands
and crying to thee: "Hosanna: blessed art thou, for thou hast
come to save the world."   Byzantine Matins

A S Jesus came near and saw the city, he wept over it,
saying, "If you, even you, had only recognized on this
day the things that make for peace! But now they are hidden
from your eyes."   Luke 19:41–42

J ERUSALEM, Jerusalem, how often have I desired to gather
your children together as a hen gathers her brood under her
wings, and you were not willing! See, your house is left to you,
desolate. For I tell you, you will not see me again until you say,
"Blessed is the one who comes in the name of the Lord."   Matthew 23:37–39

WE are told how Jesus wept for the people of Jerusalem and said he wished he could gather them under his wings like a mother hen gathers her chicks. Perhaps from that story comes a folk custom out of the Netherlands which we have adopted as our own.

The day before Palm Sunday, we make little bread-dough chicks from a favorite bread recipe. We form a little bun, pinch out a beak and poke in a currant or raisin for the eye. These little bun-chicks we then hoist on a stick or dowel and decorate with streaming ribbons and palms or branches indigenous to our gardens.

In our community many families make these processional Palm Sunday chicks and take them to Mass that morning. I know another community where it has evolved into tradition that the children bring their bread chicks, the teenagers make banners and fluttering flags of lenten purples, reds, pinks and fuchsias, and the adults bring leafy boughs decorating a little pole, or branches of olive and palms.

We are a marvelously human lot, and our feeling and passion were never meant to be checked at the church doors. If sports can bring thousands to shouting and waving flags and banners, what is it about our church-related rituals that make so many reticent and self-conscious? Liturgy is exactly concerned with what is most human about us. Theology and history do not tell us everything we need to know about religion. Beyond the rational, ritual and symbol allow us to risk powerful expressions of feelings within the safety of a discipline or form. The liturgy of these holy days must tap also our deepest and most human place, the feelings of the human heart.

Gertrud Mueller Nelson

THE branches that are blessed and brought home on Passion Sunday are placed near the cross and scriptures. They remind us that Lent is the slow coming of spring to the earth, the renewal of life. They are like the great "Hosanna" with which we hail the crucified and risen Lord.

Catholic Household Blessings and Prayers

JESUS, again greatly disturbed, came to the tomb. It was a cave, and a stone was lying against it. Jesus said, "Take away the stone." Martha, the sister of the dead man, said to him, "Lord, already there is a stench because he has been dead four days." Jesus said to her, "Did I not tell you that if you believed, you would see the glory of God?"

John 11:38–40

WE are told that when Jesus heard that Lazarus was sick, he remained where he was for two days. You see how he gives full scope to death. He grants free reign to the grave; he allows corruption to set in. He prohibits neither putrefaction nor stench from taking their normal course; he allows the realm of darkness to seize his friend, drag him down to the underworld, and take possession of him. He acts like this so that human hope may perish entirely and human despair reach its lowest depths.

Peter Chrysologus
Fifth century

THERE are often sincere, high-minded Christians, whose sound and otherwise pure faith—for it is unshaken in trials—is lacking just in this matter: they believe in the light, but as they would believe in the existence of a world never to be seen by them, or which they expect to visit at some date so distant that it seems unreal. They have a deep-seated faith, but hardly it has grown beyond the roots, since it is divorced from hope.

By his words "I am the resurrection and the life" Jesus condemns the mistake of faith without hope. He himself is its living refutation, because, in this divine incarnate person, he is the incursion of the invisible world. He *is* the resurrection and the life. Faith is directed to him, to that penetration of the unseen into the visible perpetuated in his existence, and not at an invisible world forever separated from the visible. In this way, the believer is placed by faith in possession of hope to share in the resurrection and the life, believing in them not as unattainable realities but put within reach.

Louis Bouyer

THEY took away the stone from the tomb. And Jesus looked upward and said, "Father, I thank you for having heard me. I knew that you always hear me, but I have said this for the sake of the crowd standing here, so that they may believe that you sent me." When he had said this, he cried with a loud voice, "Lazarus, come out!" The dead man came out, his hands and feet bound with strips of cloth, and his face wrapped in a cloth. Jesus said to them, "Unbind him, and let him go."

John 11:41–44

BEFORE your death, O Christ,
you have raised from death Lazarus,
who was four days dead,
and have shaken the dominion of death.
Through this one man whom you loved,
you have foretold the deliverance of all from corruption!

Byzantine Vespers

LORD Jesus,
by raising Lazarus from the dead
you showed that you came that we might have life
and have it more abundantly.

Free from the grasp of death
those who await your life-giving sacraments
and deliver them from the spirit of corruption.

*Rite of Christian
Initiation of Adults*

WE do not celebrate merely a Christ who rose without us. During Lent we are empowered to rise with him to a new life—to become precisely those new people needed today in our country. We should not just seek changes in structures because new structures are worth nothing when there are no new people to manage them and live in them.

Oscar Arnulfo Romero

O dry bones, hear the word of the LORD. I will cause breath to enter you, and you shall live. I will lay sinews on you, and will cause flesh to come upon you, and cover you with skin, and put breath in you, and you shall live; and you shall know that I am the LORD.

Ezekiel 37:4–6

G OD of all consolation,
by your just decree our bodies return to the dust
from which they were shaped,
yet in your way of mercy
you have turned this condition of darkness and death
into a proof of your loving care.
In your providence you assured Abraham,
      our father in faith,
of a burial place in the land of promise.
You extolled your servant Tobit
for his charity in burying the dead.
You willed that your own Son be laid to rest in a new tomb,
so that he might rise from it, the victor over death,
and offer us the pledge of our own resurrection.

Grant that this cemetery,
placed under the sign of the cross,
may, by the power of your blessing,
be a place of rest and hope.
May the bodies buried here sleep in your peace,
to rise immortal at the coming of your Son.
May this place be a comfort to the living,
a sign of their hope for unending life.
May prayers be offered here continually
in supplication for those who sleep in Christ
and in constant praise of your mercy.

*Order of
Christian Funerals*

Sixth
Week
of
Lent

Psalm 24:9

LIFT up, O gates, your lintels; reach up, you ancient portals,
that the king of glory may come in.

YOUR solemn processions are seen, O God,
    the procession of my God, my King,
        into the sanctuary—
the singers in front, the musicians last,
Psalm 68:24–25   between them girls playing tambourines.

WHAN that Aprill with his shoures soote
The droghte of March hath perced to the roote,
And bathed every veyne in swich licour
Of which vertu engendred is the flour;
Whan Zephirus eek with his sweete breeth
Inspired hath in every holt and heeth
The tendre croppes, and the yonge sonne
Hath in the Ram his halve cours yronne,
And smale foweles maken melodye,
That slepen al the nyght with open ye
(So priketh hem nature in hir corages);
Thanne longen folk to goon on pilgrimages.

Geoffrey Chaucer
Fourteenth century

APRIL prepares her green traffic light and the world thinks
Go.

Christopher Morley

OPEN to me the gates of righteousness,
that I may enter through them
and give thanks to the LORD.

This is the gate of the LORD;
the righteous shall enter through it.
Save us, we beseech you, O LORD!
O LORD, we beseech you, give us success!

Blessed is the one who comes in the name of the LORD.
We bless you from the house of the LORD.
The LORD is God,
and has given us light.
Bind the festal procession with branches,
up to the horns of the altar.

Psalm 118:19–20,
25–27

A s the eleventh hour draws near, that particular passage from Scripture is read in which the children bearing palms and branches came forth to meet the Lord, saying: "Blessed is the one who comes in the name of the Lord." The bishop and all the people rise immediately, and then everyone walks down from the top of the Mount of Olives, with the people preceding the bishop and responding continually with "Blessed is the one who comes in the name of the Lord" to the hymns and antiphons. All the children who are present here, including those who are not yet able to walk because they are too young and therefore are carried on their parents' shoulders, all of them bear branches, some carrying palms, others, olive branches. And the bishop is led in the same manner as the Lord once was led. From the top of the mountain as far as the city, and from there through the entire city as far as the *Anastasis,* everyone accompanies the bishop the whole way on foot, and this includes distinguished ladies and men of consequence, reciting the responses all the while.

Egeria
Fourth century

I N the tenth century in south Germany the people used to pull along with them a statue, mounted on wheels, of our Lord riding on an ass. It was called the *Palmesel* (palm-donkey) and remained in use here and there until quite recent times.

Josef Jungmann

B ISHOP Theodulph is said to have been confined for a time by Louis the Debonair, son and successor of Charlemagne, in a prison at Angers, during which time the hymn "Gloria, laus" is said to have been written. The story states that the bishop sang the new hymn from his dungeon window as the emperor was passing to the cathedral on Palm Sunday, in the year 821, and that as a result the bishop was liberated from his captivity. The hymn is still used in the church as a processional hymn on Palm Sunday.

Daniel Joseph Donahoe

G LORIA, laus, et honor tibi sit,
  Rex Christe Redemptor:
Cui puerile decus prompsit
  Hosanna pium.

A LL glory, laud, and honor
  To thee, Redeemer King:
To whom the lips of children
  Made sweet hosannas ring.

Theodulph
Ninth century

C UM angelis et pueris fideles inveniamur, triumphatori
  mortis clamantes: Hosanna in excelsis.

Look for us, the faithful, with the angels and the children,
loudly praising the conqueror of death: Hosanna in the
highest.

Monastic liturgy

T HE blind and the lame came to Jesus in the temple, and he
  cured them. But when the chief priests and the scribes
saw the amazing things that he did, and heard the children
crying out in the temple, "Hosanna to the Son of David," they
became angry and said to him, "Do you hear what these are
saying?" Jesus said to them, "Yes; have you never read,
    'Out of the mouths of infants and nursing babies
      you have prepared praise for yourself'?"

Matthew 21:14–16

A city revolted against its ruler. The King set forth to subdue and punish it, and the city hastened to request a pardon. At a distance from the city, the elders and great came and begged forgiveness. "For your sake," the King said, "I forgive one-half the guilt." At the gates of the city, the masses turned out and pleaded for mercy. "For your sake," the King said, "I forgive half the guilt that is left." When he entered the city and found all the little children gathered with song and dance and joy to appear before him, he exclaimed: "For your sake, I forgive everything!"—and the King joined in their celebration.

Jewish midrash

KING Jesus rides on a milk white horse.
No one works like him!
The river Jordan he did cross.
  No one works like him!

My Jesus left his throne above.
  No one works like him!
See his mercy and his love.
  No one works like him!

  Ride on, King Jesus!
  No one can a-hinder you.
  Ride on, King Jesus, ride on!
  No one can a-hinder you.

African-American spiritual

F AIR and eloquent flowers
     have the children strewn before the King:
the donkey was garlanded with them,
    the path was filled with them;
they scattered praises like flowers,
    their songs of joy like lilies.
Now too at this festival
    does the crowd of children scatter for you, Lord,
praises like blossoms.
    Blessed is he who was acclaimed by young children.

It is as though our hearing embraced
    an armful of children's voices,
while chaste songs, Lord,
    fill the bosoms of our ears.
Let each of us gather up a posy of such flowers,
    and with these let all intersperse
blossoms from their own piece of land,
    so that, for this great feast,
we may plait a great garland.
    Blessed is he who invited us to plait it!

Let the chief pastor weave together
    his homilies like flowers,
let the priests make a garland of their ministry,
    the deacons of their reading,
strong young men of their jubilant shouts,
    children of their psalms,
young women of their songs,
    chief citizens of their benefactions,
ordinary folk of their manner of life.

Blessed is he who gave us
        so many opportunities for good!

Ephrem
Fourth century

Y OU shall take the fruit of majestic trees, branches of palm trees, boughs of leafy trees, and willows of the brook; and you shall rejoice before the LORD your God.

Leviticus 23:40

W E were passing a pushcart vendor selling sprigs of dogwood. I had brought plenty of that from the country this morning. I asked Stein, after another silence, whether he had ever heard the legend that the cross had been made of dogwood and that supposedly explained the cross shaped vaguely into the grain of its heartwood, like that on the back of the Sardinian donkey for its having borne Our Lord into Jerusalem on his triumphal day. Stein said that he had never heard of that. I myself would never chop down a dogwood in order to check on the legend, or imagine that it would survive close scrutiny. But for the yearning spirit there is in any case another, that Christ miraculously guaranteed to the flowering tree that it would never again grow to a size great enough to hew a cross from.

Peter DeVries

O UR Lord comes from the Mount of Olives to plant young olive trees by his power from on high. Their mother is that Jerusalem which is above. And on this mountain is the heavenly Farmer.

Ambrose of Milan
Fourth century

A S Jesus rode along, people kept spreading their cloaks on the road. As he was now approaching the path down from the Mount of Olives, the whole multitude of the disciples began to praise God joyfully with a loud voice for all the deeds of power that they had seen.

Luke 19:36–37

IT is ourselves that we must spread under Christ's feet, not coats or lifeless branches or shoots of trees, matter which wastes away and delights the eye only for a few brief hours. But we have clothed ourselves with Christ's grace, with the whole Christ—"for as many of you as were baptized into Christ have put on Christ"—so let us spread ourselves like coats under his feet.

Andrew of Crete
Eighth century

LIKE splendid palm branches,
we are strewn in the Lord's path.

Latin antiphon

FOR the church, the many abuses of human life, liberty and dignity are a heartfelt suffering. The church, entrusted with the earth's glory, believes that in each person is the Creator's image and that everyone who tramples it offends God. As the holy defender of God's rights and of God's images, the church must cry out. It takes as spittle in its face, as lashes on its back, as the cross in its passion, all that human beings suffer, even though they be unbelievers. They suffer as God's images. There is no dichotomy between humans and God's image. Whoever tortures a human being, whoever abuses a human being, whoever outrages a human being abuses God's image, and the church takes as its own that cross, that martyrdom.

Oscar Arnulfo Romero

ONE who has surrendered to it knows that the way ends on the Cross—even when it is leading through the jubilation of Gennesaret or the triumphal entry into Jerusalem.

Dag Hammarskjöld

PASSING from one divine feast to another,
from palms and branches,
let us now make haste, O faithful,
to the solemn and saving celebration of Christ's passion.
Let us behold him undergo voluntary suffering for our sake,
and let us sing to him with thanksgiving a fitting hymn:
Fountain of tender mercy and haven of salvation,

Byzantine Vespers   O Lord, glory to you!

RIDE on, ride on in majesty!
Hear all the tribes hosanna cry;
O Savior meek, pursue your road
With palms and scattered garments strowed.

Ride on, ride on in majesty!
In lowly pomp ride on to die.
O Christ, your triumphs now begin
O'er captive death and conquered sin.

Ride on, ride on in majesty!
The winged squadrons of the sky
Look down with sad and wond'ring eyes
To see the approaching sacrifice.

Ride on, ride on in majesty!
Your last and fiercest strife is nigh.
The Father on his sapphire throne
Awaits his own anointed Son.

Ride on, ride on in majesty!
In lowly pomp ride on to die.
Henry Hart Milman   Bow your meek head to mortal pain,
Nineteenth century   Then take, O Christ, your pow'r and reign!

MARY took a liter of costly perfumed oil made from genuine aromatic nard and anointed the feet of Jesus and dried them with her hair; the house was filled with the fragrance of the oil.

John 12:3

SAMUEL said to Jesse, "Are all your sons here?" And he said, "There remains yet the youngest, but he is keeping the sheep." And Samuel said to Jesse, "Send and bring him; for we will not sit down until he comes here." He sent and brought him in. Now he was ruddy, and had beautiful eyes, and was handsome. The LORD said, "Rise and anoint him; for this is the one." Then Samuel took the horn of oil, and anointed him in the presence of his brothers; and the spirit of the LORD came mightily upon David from that day forward.

1 Samuel 16:11–13

HERE is my servant, whom I uphold,
    my chosen, in whom my soul delights;
I have put my spirit upon him;
    he will bring forth justice to the nations.
He will not cry or lift up his voice,
    or make it heard in the street;
a bruised reed he will not break,
    and a dimly burning wick he will not quench;
    he will faithfully bring forth justice.
He will not grow faint or be crushed
    until he has established justice in the earth;
    and the coastlands wait for his teaching.

Isaiah 42:1–4

S AID Judas to Mary, "Now what will you do
With your ointment so rich and so rare?"
"I'll pour it all over the feet of the Lord,
    And I'll wipe it away with my hair," she said,
    "I'll wipe it away with my hair."

"Oh Mary, O Mary, O think of the poor.
    This ointment it could have been sold;
And think of the blankets and think of the bread
    You could buy with the silver and gold," he said,
    "You could buy with the silver and gold."

"Tomorrow, tomorrow, I'll think of the poor;
    Tomorrow," she said, "not today;
For dearer than all of the poor in the world
    Is my love who is going away," she said,
    "My love who is going away."

Said Jesus to Mary, "Your love is so deep
    Today, you may do as you will.
Tomorrow, you say, I am going away,
    But my body I leave with you still," he said,
    "My body I leave with you still."

"The poor of the world are my body," he said,
    "To the end of the world they shall be.
The bread and the blankets you give to the poor
    You'll know you have given to me," he said,
    "You'll know you have given to me."

"My body will hang on the cross of the world
    Tomorrow," he said, "not today.
And Martha and Mary will find me again
    And wash all my sorrow away," he said,
Sydney Carter   "And wash all my sorrow away."

I⊤ is no accident that chrism, the noblest of the three oils, should be used for the sign of the cross in confirmation. Chrism is produced by adding aromatic essences (especially balsam) to olive oil. Here again the element of public mani-festation that is proper to confirmation exercises its influence. Paul says of Christians that they should be "the aroma of Christ" (2 Corinthians 2:14). Wherever Christians live their baptism and confirmation in an authentic way, they emit as it were a "strong and wholesome fragrance."   Balthasar Fischer

H⊤S voice as the sound of the dulcimer sweet,
    Is heard thro' the shadows of death;
The cedars of Lebanon bow at his feet,
    The air is perfumed with his breath.
His lips as the fountain of righteousness flow,
    That waters the garden of grace;
From which their salvation the Gentiles shall know,
    And bask in the smiles of his face.

O! thou in whose presence my soul takes delight,
    On whom, in affliction, I call;
My comfort by day, and my song in the night,
    My hope, my salvation, my all —
Where dost thou at noontide resort with thy sheep,
    To feed on the pastures of love?
Say why in the valley of death should I weep,
    Or alone in th' wilderness rove?

O! why should I wander an alien from thee,
    And cry in the desert for bread?
Thy foes will rejoice when my sorrows they see,
    And smile at the tears I have shed.
Ye daughters of Zion, declare, have you seen
    The Star that on Israel shone?
Say where in your tents my beloved has been,
    And where, with his flock, he is gone?

The roses of Sharon, the lilies that grow
   In the vales, on the banks of the streams,
On his cheeks in the beauty of excellence blow,
   And his eyes are as quivers of beams.
His voice as the sound of the dulcimer sweet,
   Is heard through the shadows of death;
The cedars of Lebanon bow at his feet,
   The air is perfumed with his breath.

The Southern Harmony

Exodus 30:22–25

TAKE the finest spices: of liquid myrrh five hundred shekels, and of sweet-smelling cinnamon half as much, that is, two hundred fifty, and two hundred fifty of aromatic cane, and five hundred of cassia—measured by the sanctuary shekel—and a *hin* of olive oil; and you shall make of these a sacred anointing oil blended as by the perfumer.

O Redeemer, receive the song of those
   who sing your praise.
A tree made fruitful by the fostering light of the sun
      brought forth this oil that it might be blessed.
Humbly we bring it to the Savior of the world.
In your kindness, O King of the eternal homeland,
Consecrate this oil of olives as a sign of life,
      a safeguard against the demon.
May both men and women be made new
      by being anointed by the chrism,
And may the wound to their glorious dignity be healed.
Our minds being cleansed at the sacred font,
      let our sins be put to flight;
May holy gifts be lavished on those
      whose foreheads are anointed.
You who were born from the heart of the Father,
      and did fill the womb of the Virgin,

Grant light, put an end to death for those who share
in the chrism.
May this day be a festival for us for ever and ever:
May it be made holy with worthy praise,
and may it not grow old with time.

Latin hymn at the
consecration of chrism

WHEN they came from Bethany, Jesus was hungry. Seeing in the distance a fig tree in leaf, he went to see
whether perhaps he would find anything on it. When he came
to it, he found nothing but leaves, for it was not the season for
figs. He said to it, "May no one ever eat fruit from you again."
And his disciples heard it. The next morning as they passed by,
they saw the fig tree withered away to its roots.

Mark 11:12–14, 20

WOE is me! There is no first-ripe fig for which I hunger.
The faithful have disappeared from the land,
and there is no one left who is upright;
they all lie in wait for blood,
and they hunt each other with nets.
Their hands are skilled to do evil;
the official and the judge ask for a bribe,
and the powerful dictate what they desire;
thus they pervert justice.
The best of them is like a brier,
the most upright of them a thorn hedge.
The day of their sentinels, of their punishment, has come;
now their confusion is at hand.

Micah 7:1–4

O brothers and sisters,
let us fear the punishment of the fig tree,
withered because it was unfruitful;
and let us bring worthy fruits of repentance
unto Christ our God, who grants us great mercy.

Byzantine Matins

Byzantine Matins

THINK, wretched soul, upon the hour of the end; recall with fear how the fig tree withered. Work diligently with the talent that is given to thee; be vigilant and cry aloud: May we not be left outside the bridal chamber of Christ!

WHEN the church is reborn of water in this same Spirit, she becomes one body in Christ, so that they are two in a single body.

This wedding lasts from the first moment of Christ's incarnation until his return, so that all its rites may be completed. Then those who are ready, having duly fulfilled the requirements of so exalted a marriage, will go in to the eternal wedding banquet with Christ, filled with awe. Meanwhile, Christ's promised bride is brought to her husband, and in faith and mercy they pledge themselves to one another every day until he comes again.

Paschasius Radbertus
Ninth century

NOW John's disciples and the Pharisees were fasting; and people came and said to Jesus, "Why do John's disciples and the disciples of the Pharisees fast, but your disciples do not fast?" Jesus said to them, "The wedding guests cannot fast while the bridegroom is with them, can they? As long as they have the bridegroom with them, they cannot fast. The days will come when the bridegroom is taken away from them, and then they will fast on that day.

Mark 2:18–20

L ET those of us who have wisely finished
the course of fasting
and who celebrate with love the beginning
    of the suffering of the Passion of the Lord,
Let us fear the sterility of the fig tree;
    let us dry up through almsgiving the sweetness
        of passion.
In order that we may joyously anticipate the resurrection,
    let us procure like myrrh pardon from on high   Romanos
    because the eye that never sleeps observes all things.   Sixth century

I T is zeal for your house that has consumed me;
the insults of those who insult you have fallen on me.
When I humbled my soul with fasting,
    they insulted me for doing so.
When I made sackcloth my clothing,
    I became a byword to them.
I am the subject of gossip for those who sit in the gate,
    and the drunkards make songs about me.

But as for me, my prayer is to you, O LORD.
    At an acceptable time, O God,
    in the abundance of your steadfast love, answer me.   Psalm 69:9–13

T HEY came to Jerusalem. And Jesus entered the temple and
began to drive out those who were selling and those who
were buying in the temple, and he overturned the tables of
the money changers and the seats of those who sold doves;
and he would not allow anyone to carry anything through
the temple.   Mark 11:15–16

L ORD our God,
holy is your name!
Incline our hearts to your commandments,
and give us the wisdom of the cross,
so that, freed from sin,
which imprisons us in our own self-centeredness,
we may be open to the gift of your Spirit,
Italian sacramentary   and so become living temples of your love.

I have come,
And I've not come in vain.
I have come to sweep
The house of the Lord.
Clean, clean, for I've come,
And I've not come in vain.

With my broom in my hand,
With my fan and my flail,
This work I will do,
And I will not fail,
For lo! I have come,
Shaker hymn   And I've not come in vain.

S PRING is the usual period for housecleaning and removing
the dust and dirt which, notwithstanding all precautions,
Mrs. Beeton's   will accumulate during the winter months from dust, smoke,
Household Management   gas, etc.

M ONDAY through Wednesday of Holy Week are tradi-
tionally the days for "spring housecleaning." We put
up freshly washed curtains, polish some silver in anticipation
of the Easter festivities, wax the woodwork or turn the mat-
tress: anything that shares in and points up our spiritual new
life. We own little silver or copper, but in our house it has
become something of a treat to haul out the silver teaspoons
and the copper kettle that need a shine and put them into use
again for the feast of Easter. Polishing away the tarnish is
graphic and rewarding.

Gertrud Mueller Nelson

O RIGINALLY the washing of the altar was a utilitarian rite
whose purpose was to clean the whole church in
preparation for the celebration of the Easter festival. Thus
Isidore of Seville speaks of the altars, walls, floors and vessels
being washed on Maundy Thursday. This statement is juxta-
posed to one referring to the Lord's washing of his disciples'
feet, thus discreetly suggesting a symbolism: the church in the
person of the disciples is washed, cleansed from sin. . . . The
rite is performed in Rome by seven canons of St. Peter's after
the last office of Maundy Thursday. With the other clergy of
the basilica, they go in procession to the Altar of the Confession. Psalm 22 is intoned and the canons then pour wine
mixed with water on the altar. The cardinal archpriest
approaches and with a branch of yew spreads it over the altar
and the canons do likewise. Afterwards, they dry the altar
with sponges and towels.

J. D. Crichton

A CCORDING to immemorial Carmelite usage, on Holy
Thursday roses or other flowers are strewn on the high
altar after it has been washed.

Archdale A. King

V ISIT this house, O Lord; keep the devil's wily influence away
from it. Let your holy angels dwell here, to guard us in
peace. And let your blessing rest upon us always.

Missal of Pius V

THIS day shall be a day of remembrance for you. You shall celebrate it as a festival to the LORD; throughout your generations you shall observe it as a perpetual ordinance. Seven days you shall eat unleavened bread; on the first day you shall remove leaven from your houses, for whoever eats leavened bread from the first day until the seventh day shall be cut off from Israel.

Exodus 12:14–15

CHAMETZ (leavened bread) became a symbol of what is allowed to stand around. *Chametz* signified staleness and deadening routine; getting rid of it became the symbol of freshness and growth. Since Passover occurs in the spring, the total cleaning of the house to eliminate leaven was easily expanded to a comprehensive spring-cleaning. Throwing out accumulated staleness and the dead hand of winter, cleaning the house and changing utensils became a psychological backdrop for reenacting emancipation. Thus, housecleaning became part of a cosmic process.

Irving Greenberg

SO intense are these spring housecleaning activities that Iraqi women have called Passover *"az frihli"*—"the festival of falling apart."

Mae Shafter Rockland

THEY were taught to care for the most distant in the most immediate, knowing that the passing is a reflection of the lasting, that tables in their humble homes may become consecrated altars, that a single deed of one may decide the fate of all. Characteristic of their piety was the unheroic sacrifice— unassuming, inconspicuous devotion rather than extravagance, mortification, asceticism. The purpose was to ennoble the common, to endow worldly things with hieratic beauty.

Abraham Joshua Heschel

F ATHER,
through your holy prophets
you proclaimed to all who draw near you,
"Wash and be cleansed,"
and through Christ you have granted us rebirth in the Spirit.

Bless these your servants
as they earnestly prepare for baptism.

Fulfill your promise:
sanctify them in preparation for your gifts,
that they may come to be reborn as your children
and enter the community of your church.

*Rite of Christian
Initiation of Adults*

F ROM my mother's womb you are my strength.

Psalm 71:6

N OW that you have purified your souls by your obedience
to the truth so that you have genuine mutual love, love
one another deeply from the heart. You have been born anew.

1 Peter 1:22–23

P ERHAPS God is strong enough to exult in monotony. It is
possible that God says every morning, "Do it again" to the
sun; and every evening, "Do it again" to the moon. It may not
be automatic necessity that makes all daisies alike; it may be
that God makes every daisy separately, but has never gotten
tired of making them. It may be that God has the eternal
appetite of infancy.

G. K. Chesterton

W HY have you forgotten us completely?
Why have you forsaken us these many days?
Restore us to yourself, O LORD, that we may be restored;
renew our days as of old.

Lamentations 5:20–21

W HEN in the future your child asks you, "What does this
mean?" you shall answer, "By strength of hand the
LORD brought us out of Egypt, from the house of slavery."

Exodus 13:14

N OT only our ancestors alone did the Holy One redeem
but *us* as well, along with them, as it is written: "And
God freed *us* from Egypt so as to take us and give us the land
which had been sworn to our ancestors."

Therefore, let us rejoice at the wonder of our deliverance:
from bondage to freedom, from agony to joy, from mourning
to festivity, from darkness to light, from servitude to redemption. Before God let us ever sing a new song.

The Passover
Haggadah

H AD God brought us out of Egypt
and not divided the sea for us, *dayenu!*
Had God divided the sea
and not permitted us to cross on dry land, *dayenu!*
Had God permitted us to cross the sea on dry land
and not sustained us in the desert, *dayenu!*
Had God sustained us for forty years in the desert
and not fed us with manna, *dayenu!*
Had God fed us with manna
and not given us the Sabbath, *dayenu!*
Had God given us the Sabbath
and not brought us to Mount Sinai, *dayenu!*
Had God brought us to Mount Sinai
and not given us the Torah, *dayenu!*

Had God given us the Torah
   and not led us into the land of Israel, *dayenu!*
Had God led us into the land of Israel
   and not built for us the Temple, *dayenu!*
Had God built for us the Temple
   and not sent us prophets of truth, *dayenu!*
Had God sent us prophets of truth
   and not made us a holy people, *dayenu!*

Passover song
Dayenu means
"I would be content."

G OD, of your goodness give me yourself for you are
   sufficient for me. I cannot properly ask anything less, to
be worthy of you. If I were to ask less, I should always be in
want. In you alone do I have all.

Julian of Norwich
Fourteenth century

I am content! My Jesus ever lives,
   In whom my heart is pleased.
He has fulfilled the law of God for me,
   God's wrath he has appeased.
Since he in death could perish never,
   I also shall not die forever.
I am content! I am content!

I am content! At length I shall be free,
   Awakened from the dead,
Arising glorious evermore to be
   With you, my living head.
My Lord, earth's binding fetters sever,
   Then shall my soul rejoice forever.
I am content! I am content!

Johann J. Möller
Seventeenth century

THE suffering and death of your Son
brought life to the whole world,
moving our hearts to praise your glory.
The power of the cross reveals your judgment on this world
and the kingship of Christ crucified.

Roman rite

WHEN Christ came as a high priest of the good things that
have come, then through the greater and perfect tent
(not made with hands, that is, not of this creation), he entered
once for all into the Holy Place, not with the blood of goats
and calves, but with his own blood, thus obtaining eternal
redemption.

For this reason he is the mediator of a new covenant, so that
those who are called may receive the promised eternal
inheritance, because a death has occurred that redeems them
from the transgressions under the first covenant. Where a will
is involved, the death of the one who made it must be
established. For a will takes effect only at death, since it is not
in force as long as the one who made it is alive.

Hebrews 9:11–12,
15–17

MY song is love unknown,
My Savior's love to me,
Love to the loveless shown
That they might lovely be.
Oh, who am I
That for my sake
My Lord should take
Frail flesh and die,
My Lord should take
Frail flesh and die?

Samuel Crossman
Seventeenth century

I N judging our salvation or definitive damnation, God will not be guided by cultic criteria—when and how we prayed—not by doctrinal criteria—what truths we believe in. God will be guided by ethical criteria: what we did for others. The eternal destiny of human beings will be measured by how much or how little solidarity we have displayed with the hungry, the thirsty, the naked, and the oppressed. In the end we will be judged in terms of love.

Leonardo Boff

A BOVE all else the South African song is a victory-song, a defiant hymn.

This song sounds out when two thousand women and children gather on a sandy field outside Capetown. They refuse to be separated from their menfolk and sent to Transkei, a "homeland" a thousand miles away, where starvation and sickness await them, a reserve that many have never been in, but which is now according to the apartheid policy the only legal domicile for these women. Despite constant harassment from the police, despite the cold and rain the women stand there round the fires and the wooden cross—and sing hymns. After six weeks of unbroken singing, the patience of the police ends. Early one morning, just before dawn, they strike. Heavily armed and with dogs they occupy the small hills around the camp. The women gather round the cross, fall to their knees in the wet sand and pray. Then they dance round the cross, the symbol of this folly. These women have lost everything—their homes, their families, their jobs and their possessions. They have nothing more to lose—only their chains, but everything to win.

Anders Nyberg

S IMEON blessed them and said to his mother Mary, "This child is destined for the falling and the rising of many in Israel, and to be a sign that will be opposed so that the inner thoughts of many will be revealed—and a sword will pierce your own soul too."

Luke 2:34–35

Pity me, young and old,
a celebration of blood has come upon us;
I had but one son,
and I weep for him.

O my son, sweet, singled out,
share your sufferings with your mother;
I bore you close to my heart, dear son,
and served you truly.
Speak to your mother, console my grief;
now that you are deserting me and all my dearest hopes.

O my little son, if I had you closer,
I would help you somehow:
your dear head hangs awry, I would support it;
blood flows from you, I would cleanse it away;
you cry for water, I would give you to drink
but I cannot reach your holy body.

O angel Gabriel,
where is that joy
of which you promised me so much,
saying: O Virgin thou art filled with love!
Yet I am filled with grief,
my body has rotted within me, and all my bones.

Implore God, you sweet and mourning mothers,
that such a fate may never befall your children,
which I, a poor woman, now witness
befalling my beloved son,
as he suffers torment, yet is guiltless.

I have no other and shall have no other son,
Polish hymn   only you, stretched upon the cross.

A T the Cross her station keeping,
Stood the mournful Mother weeping,
Close to Jesus to the last.

Through her heart, his sorrow sharing,
All his bitter anguish bearing,
Now at length the sword had passed.

Holy Mother! pierce me through;
In my heart each wound renew
Of my Savior crucified.

Let me mingle tears with thee,
Mourning him who mourned for me,
All the days that I may live.

Let me, to my latest breath,
In my body bear the death
Of that dying Son of thine.

Christ, when thou shalt call me hence,
Be thy Mother my defence,
Be thy Cross my victory;

While my body here decays,
May my soul thy goodness praise,
Safe in paradise with thee.

Latin hymn
Seventeenth century

I lie in my bed
As I would lie in the grave,
Thine arm beneath my neck,
    Thou Son of Mary victorious.

Celtic prayer

U PON my bed at night
   I sought him whom my soul loves;
I sought him, but found him not;
   I called him, but he gave no answer.
"I will rise now and go about the city,
   in the streets and in the squares;
I will seek him whom my soul loves."
   I sought him, but found him not.
The sentinels found me,
   as they went about in the city.
"Have you seen him whom my soul loves?"
Scarcely had I passed them,
   when I found him whom my soul loves.
I held him, and would not let him go
   until I brought him into my mother's house,
   and into the chamber of her that conceived me.
I adjure you, O daughters of Jerusalem,
   by the gazelles or the wild does:
do not stir up or awaken love
Song of Songs 3:1–5   until it is ready!

O NCE Mary would go wandering,
   To all the lands would run,
That she might find her son,
   That she might find her son.

Whom met she as she journeyed forth?
   Saint Peter, that good man,
Who sadly did her scan,
   Who sadly did her scan.

"O tell me have you seen him yet—
   The one that I love the most—
The son whom I have lost,
   The son whom I have lost?"

"Too well, too well, I've seen thy son;
 'Twas by a palace gate.
Most grievous was his state,
 Most grievous was his state."

"O say, what wore he on his head?"
 "A crown of thorns he wore;
A cross he also bore,
 A cross he also bore."

"Ah me! and he must bear that cross,
 Till he's brought to the hill,
For cruel men to kill,
 For cruel men to kill."

"Nay, Mary, cease thy weeping, dear:
 The wounds they are but small;
But heaven is won for all,
 But heaven is won for all!"   German carol

A s you chose to have the mournful mother
  stand by your Son in his agony on the cross,
grant that we too may bring love and comfort
to our brothers and sisters in distress.   Roman rite

C AN you drink the cup that I am going to drink?   Matthew 20:22

FOR in the hand of the LORD there is a cup
with foaming wine, well mixed;
God will pour a draught from it,
    and all the wicked of the earth
Psalm 75:8   shall drain it down to the dregs.

ONE of the twelve, who was called Judas Iscariot, went to
the chief priests and said, "What will you give me if I
betray him to you?" They paid him thirty pieces of silver. And
from that moment he began to look for an opportunity to
Matthew 26:14–16   betray him.

IT was on Spy Wednesday,
And all in the morning,
That Judas betrayed our dear heav'nly King:
And was not this a woeful thing?
English carol   And sweet Jesus we'll call him by name.

LOOK down, we beseech you, Lord, on your family, for
whose sake our Lord Jesus Christ did not hesitate to be
betrayed into the hands of the wicked and to undergo the
Roman rite   torment of the cross.

INSULTS have broken my heart,
so that I am in despair.
I looked for pity, but there was none;
    and for comforters, but I found none.
They gave me poison for food,
Psalm 69:20–21   and for my thirst they gave me vinegar to drink.

O gracious Shepherd! for thy simple flock
  By guileful goats to ravening wolves misled,
  Who thine own dear heart's precious blood didst shed,
And lamb-like offered to the butcher block.

Henry Constable
Sixteenth century

S TRIKE the shepherd, that the sheep may be scattered.

Zechariah 13:7

T HE prisoners in the jails of my country are not hung upside down and tortured; our poor do not die of cholera or plague. But my relation to most of the people in the world just cannot be described as exactly the one which morality would demand. And this is why I realize that as long as I preserve my loyalty to my childhood training I will never know what it is to be truly comfortable, and this is why I feel a fantastic need to tear that training out of my heart once and for all so that I can finally begin to enjoy the life that is spread out before me like a feast. And every time a friend makes that happy choice and sets himself or herself free, I find that I inwardly exult and rejoice, because it means there will be one less person to disapprove of me if I choose to do the same.

As I write these words, in New York City in 1985, more and more people who grew up around me are making this decision; they are throwing away their moral chains and learning to enjoy their true situation: Yes, they are admitting loudly and bravely, we live in beautiful homes, we're surrounded by beautiful gardens, our children are playing with wonderful toys, and our kitchen shelves are filled with wonderful food. And if there are people out there who don't seem to like us and who would like to break into our homes and take what we have, well then, part of our good fortune is that we can afford to pay guards to man our gates and keep those people away.

And if those who protect us need to hit people in the face with the butts of their rifles, or if they need perhaps even to turn around and shoot, they have our permission. . . .

The perfectly decent person who follows a certain chain of reasoning, ever so slightly and subtly incorrect, becomes a perfect monster at the end of the chain.

Wallace Shawn

J ESUS said to Judas, "Do quickly what you are going to do." Now no one at the table knew why he said this to him. Some thought that, because Judas had the common purse, Jesus was telling him, "Buy what we need for the festival"; or, that he should give something to the poor. Judas immediately went out. And it was night.

John 13:27–30

N O one can be said to have perfectly renounced the world if one still keeps the purse of opinion in the hidden recesses of one's heart.

Bonaventure
Thirteenth century

A T an acceptable time, O God,
in the abundance of your steadfast love, answer me.
With your faithful help rescue me
from sinking in the mire;
let me be delivered from my enemies
and from the deep waters.
Do not let the flood sweep over me,
or the deep swallow me up,

Psalm 69:13–15   or the Pit close its mouth over me.

H E, who navigated with success
the dangerous river of his own birth
once more set forth

on a voyage of discovery
into the land I floated on
but could not touch to claim.

His feet slid on the bank,
the currents took him;
he swirled with ice and trees in the swollen water

and plunged into distant regions,
his head a bathysphere;
through his eyes' thin glass bubbles

he looked out, reckless adventurer
on a landscape stranger than Uranus
we have all been to and some remember.

There was an accident; the air locked,
he was hung in the river like a heart.
They retrieved the swamped body,

cairn of my plans and future charts,
with poles and hooks
from among the nudging logs.

It was spring, the sun kept shining, the new grass
leapt to solidity;
my hands glistened with details.

After the long trip I was tired of waves.
My foot hit rock. The dreamed sails
collapsed, ragged.
    I planted him in this country
    like a flag.   Margaret Atwood

Death, like an overflowing stream,
Sweeps us away; our life's a dream,
An empty tale, a morning flow'r,
Cut down and wither'd in an hour.

Early American hymn

One only has explored
The deepmost; but he did not die of it.
Not yet, not yet he died. Our human Lord
Touched the extreme; it is not infinite.

But over the abyss
Of God's capacity for woe he stayed
One hesitating hour; what gulf was this?
Forsaken he went down, and was afraid.

Alice Meynell

When Tim's head rose above the surface of the raging foam he was already close to the tunnel. He could see the waters contending, boiling, stooping as they constrained themselves into the tunnel whose entrance was below the surface. The smooth stone walls of the canal now rose high above on either side, cutting out the light of the sky. Tim thought, oh why did I have to drink this water and not the other? And he thought, oh, Gertrude, Gertrude—He was fully conscious that he was about to die. He took a last gasping breath and instinctively ducked his head into the foam as he was sucked down under the submerged center of the stone arch.

Tim had taken another breath. He was aware of the breath as a miracle, a precious amazing event. Then something hit him very hard on the head. He swallowed water, choking. He was in total darkness, at any rate if his eyes were open, which he was not sure about. With the realization that he was still alive came an instantaneous absolute death-fear identical with hope. The roof of the tunnel was at this point and for the moment and only a little way, clear of the water. Tim took another breath. All the time he was, in some sort, swimming, that is, he was agitating his limbs instinctively so as to keep his head above the surface. This was difficult since his legs seemed to have been swept below his head rather than behind it, and the strong water in the narrower space had somehow imprisoned his arms. His dabbing feet could touch no bottom below. He made a schematic effort to float on his back with his nose and mouth toward the roof, but this failed, and he received in the process a hard bang on the brow. He had already grasped the problem, which was to keep his face above water while not being stunned and rendered unconscious by a blow from the roof. His body rather than his mind informed him that it was no use. In a moment the roof would descend to the level of the water or below it, or else the whole torrent would plunge headlong into some deep hole. He would die indeed like a rat, and perhaps no one would ever know what had happened to him. No one would know and no one would care. Oh, let me live! he prayed. A little while ago he had seemed to want death, but now he desired so passionately to live. He thought, I must live, I must, I must!

The roof seemed to be descending, more and more often and more and more violently it struck him as he opened his mouth to breathe. He had by now established a rhythm, not just instinctively gasping, but taking a deep breath and holding it with his head ducked down in the water, then taking another. He even tried with one hand to gauge the height of the roof before he lifted his head to breathe. This was no help however since the darkness had deprived him of all sense of space and touch and it was difficult to maneuver his arms. Moreover his head was spinning with repeated blows and he was swallowing more water. Each time he took a breath he thought this may be the last. He thought this fear, this darkness, *is* death, this is what it's like. But, oh, I so much want to live, please let me live, any life is better than death, oh, let me only live.   Iris Murdoch

J UST as a swimmer, who with his last breath
flounders ashore from perilous seas, might turn
to memorize the wide water of his death—

So did I turn, my soul still fugitive
from death's surviving image, to stare down
that pass that none had ever left alive.

Dante Alighieri
Fourteenth century

F ATHER of life and God not of the dead but of the living,
you sent your Son to proclaim life,
to snatch us from the realm of death,
and to lead us to the resurrection.

Free these elect
from the death-dealing power of the spirit of evil,
so that they may bear witness
to their new life in the risen Christ.

*Rite of Christian
Initiation of Adults*

I have a feeling that my boat
has struck, down there in the depths,
against a great thing.
And nothing
happens! Nothing . . . Silence . . . Waves . . .
—Nothing happens? Or has everything happened,
and are we standing now, quietly, in the new life?

Juan Ramón Jiménez

I have a baptism to undergo and how I long for it to be accomplished.

Luke 12:50

JAMES and John, the sons of Zebedee, came forward to Jesus and said to him, "Teacher, we want you to do for us whatever we ask of you." And he said to them, "What is it you want me to do for you?" And they said to him, "Grant us to sit, one at your right hand and one at your left, in your glory." But Jesus said to them, "You do not know what you are asking. Are you able to drink the cup that I drink, or be baptized with the baptism that I am baptized with?" They replied, "We are able." Then Jesus said to them, "The cup that I drink you will drink; and with the baptism with which I am baptized, you will be baptized; but to sit at my right hand or at my left is not mine to grant, but it is for those for whom it has been prepared."

When the ten heard this, they began to be angry with James and John. So Jesus called them and said to them, "You know that among the Gentiles those whom they recognize as their rulers lord it over them, and their great ones are tyrants over them. But it is not so among you; but whoever wishes to become great among you must be your servant, and whoever wishes to be first among you must be slave of all. For the Son of Man came not to be served but to serve, and to give his life as a ransom for many."

Mark 10:35–45

I tol' Jesus it would be all right,
   if he changed my name.

Jesus tol' me I would have to live humble,
   if he changed my name.

Jesus tol' me that the world would be 'gainst me,
   if he changed my name.

But I tol' Jesus it would be all right—
   if he changed my name!

African-American
spiritual

G OD our Father,
you always work to save us,
and now we rejoice in the great love
you give to your chosen people.
Protect all who are about to become your children,

Roman rite   and continue to bless those who are already baptized.

T HAT is why we preach this way. We wish to shake our
baptized people out of habits that threaten to make them
practically baptized pagans, idolaters of their money and
power. What sort of baptized persons are these? Those who
want to bear the mark of the Spirit and the fire that Christ
baptizes with must take the risk of renouncing everything and

Oscar Arnulfo Romero   seeking only God's reign and justice.

W E must not expect baptism to free us from the temptations of our persecutor. The body that concealed him
made even the Word of God a target for the enemy; his
assumption of a visible form made even the Invisible Light an
object of attack. Nevertheless, since we have at hand the
means of overcoming our enemy, we must have no fear of the

Gregory of Nazianzus   struggle. Flaunt in his face the water and the Spirit!
Fourth century

M AUNDY Thursday served as a preparation for the feast of
Easter about to follow. The penitents were to be able
to join in the Easter celebrations; therefore they had to be
"reconciled" on the day before the Paschal Triduum began,

Josef Jungmann   that is, on Maundy Thursday.

THOSE that are regenerated add to our ranks; those that return, increase our numbers. There is a laver of water; there is a laver of tears. From the one, there is joy because of the admittance of them that are called; from the other, there is gladness because of them that repent.

Roman Pontifical

JESUS, I wish you would let me wash your feet, since it was through walking about in me that you soiled them. I wish you would give me the task of wiping the stains from your feet, because it was my behavior that put them there. But where can I get the running water I need to wash your feet? If I have no water, at least I have tears.

Ambrose of Milan
Fourth century

NOT by annihilating the wicked, not by forcibly eliminating evil from among humankind is righteousness to be realized; the Lord wills to rehabilitate the world by turning sinners from evil ways that they may live. And we must admit that this is more difficult than the use of force.

John L. McKenzie

I am poured out like water,
and all my bones are out of joint;
my heart is like wax;
    it is melted within my breast;
my mouth is dried up like a potsherd,
    and my tongue sticks to my jaws;
    you lay me in the dust of death.

Psalm 22:14–15

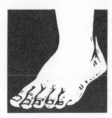

THE penitents, who were commanded to do public penance and were removed from the church at the beginning of Lent, are reconciled on Holy Thursday. The bishop is seated near the altar and with the other ministers prays the seven penitential psalms and the litany of the saints. The penitents are prostrate outside the doors of the church. They are barefoot and have unlighted candles in their hands. Part way through the litany the bishop sends two subdeacons with lighted candles. They stand at the thresholds of the church and chant: "As I live, says the Lord, I do not wish the death of sinners but that they might turn and live." The subdeacons then put out their candles and return to their places and the litany continues. Later in the litany the bishop sends two other subdeacons in the same way and they chant: "The Lord says: Do penance, for the reign of God is near." Likewise, they extinguish their candles and return to their places. At the end of the litany the bishop sends to the penitents an old deacon who holds a very large, lighted candle. At the door the deacon chants: "Lift your heads. Behold, your redemption is at hand!" and the deacon lights the candles of the penitents.

Then the bishop and all the ministers go to the middle of the church. The archdeacon continues on to the door and chants loudly to the penitents: "Stand now in silence and listen to what is said." The archdeacon turns toward the bishop and chants: "The acceptable time has come. Now is the forgiveness of sins granted and the welcoming of those reborn in grace. The waters wash, so do tears. With those reborn there is joy, for they have heard their call. With those who have done penance there is joy in their forgiveness. In their sins they have humbled themselves and cried out with the prophet: 'We have sinned, been unjust and done evil. Have mercy on us, Lord.' The gospel responds: 'Blessed are those who weep, for they shall be consoled.' These penitents have eaten the bread of sorrow, have cried their tears, have fasted—all that they might recover their lost health of spirit."

The bishop then goes to the door and speaks to the penitents about the mercy of God and about how they are to live when they have been brought back into the church. Then he chants: "Come, come, come, children and hear me. I will teach you the fear of the Lord." The penitents kneel for a short time and then rise. The invitation is repeated twice more, then the bishop goes into the church a little ways and all inside chant Psalm 34 with the antiphon: "Come to God and be enlightened, and your faces will not be ashamed." During the psalm the penitents come into the church and prostrate themselves, weeping, at the feet of the bishop. After the psalm, the bishop asks if these penitents are worthy of being reconciled. The archdeacon answers that they are, and the penitents stand. The bishop takes one of them by the hand, and all of them join hands as in a chain. The schola chants: "I say to you that there is joy among God's angels when one sinner repents." Then the bishop leads them, hand in hand, to the middle of the church.

The bishop invites all to lift up their hearts and give thanks, and so continues: "We give you thanks . . . through Christ our Lord. He willed to be born that he might pay Adam's debt to you, eternal Father, and might remove our death with his own, and bear our wounds in his body, and wash away our offences with his blood." The bishop goes on to remember the forgiveness of Peter and of the thief, and to ask that these penitents be reconciled and received at the holy meal. Everyone present then kneels or lies prostrate on the floor as psalms are chanted. Then the bishop rises and chants several prayers, ending with the absolution. Finally the bishop sprinkles the penitents with holy water and honors them with incense, saying: "Awake, sleepers, rise from the dead, and Christ will give you light." After the bishop blesses them, the reconciled penitents take off their penitential garments and put on clean clothing.

As described in the
Roman Pontifical

HAVE mercy on me, O God,
      according to your steadfast love;
according to your abundant mercy
   blot out my transgressions.
Wash me thoroughly from my iniquity,
   and cleanse me from my sin.
For I know my transgressions,
   and my sin is ever before me.
Against you, you alone, have I sinned,

and done what is evil in your sight,
so that you are justified in your sentence
    and blameless when you pass judgment.
Indeed, I was born guilty,
    a sinner when my mother conceived me.

You desire truth in the inward being;
    therefore teach me wisdom in my secret heart.
Purge me with hyssop, and I shall be clean;
    wash me, and I shall be whiter than snow.
Let me hear joy and gladness;
    let the bones that you have crushed rejoice.
Hide your face from my sins,
    and blot out all my iniquities.
Create in me a clean heart, O God,
    and put a new and right spirit within me.
Do not cast me away from your presence,
    and do not take your holy spirit from me.
Restore to me the joy of your salvation,
Psalm 51:1–12   and sustain in me a willing spirit.

LORD our God,
    you created us in love
and redeemed us in mercy.
While we were exiled from heaven
by the jealousy of the evil one,
you gave us your only Son,
who shed his blood to save us.
Send now your Holy Spirit
to breathe new life into your children,
for you do not want us to die
but to live for you alone.
You do not abandon those who abandon you;
correct us as a Father
and restore us to your family.

Lord,
your sons and daughters stand before you
in humility and trust.
Look with compassion on us
as we confess our sins.
Heal our wounds;
stretch out a hand of pity
to save us and raise us up.
Keep us free from harm
as members of Christ's body,
as sheep of your flock,
as children of your family.
Do not allow the enemy
to triumph over us
or death to claim us for ever,
for you raised us to new life in baptism.

Hear, Lord, the prayers we offer from contrite hearts.
Have pity on us as we acknowledge our sins.
Lead us back to the way of holiness.
Protect us now and always
from the wounds of sin.
May we ever keep safe in all its fullness
the gift your love once gave us
and your mercy now restores.

Rite of Penance

THE firstfruits of the Lord's Passion fill this present day with
light. Come then, all who love to keep the feast, and let us
welcome it with songs. For the Creator draws near to undergo
the cross.

Byzantine Matins

O N the first day of Unleavened Bread, when the Passover lamb is sacrificed, Jesus' disciples said to him, "Where do you want us to go and make the preparations for you to eat the Passover?" So he sent two of his disciples, saying to them, "Go into the city, and a man carrying a jar of water will meet you; follow him, and wherever he enters, say to the owner of the house, 'The Teacher asks, Where is my guest room where I may eat the Passover with my disciples?' He will show you a large room upstairs, furnished and ready. Make preparations for us there." So the disciples set out and went to the city, and found everything as he had told them; and they prepared the Passover meal.

Mark 14:12–16

T HE LORD said to Moses and Aaron in the land of Egypt: This month shall mark for you the beginning of months; it shall be the first month of the year for you.

Exodus 12:1–2

T HE gentiles are greatly mistaken in thinking that January is the first month: Moses was right in saying that the Pasch was the first month, for now the herbs in the meadows rise, as it were, from death; likewise the trees begin to bloom, and the first buds appear on the vines. The very air is joyful with this newness of time, a season when the elements of the earth are renewed. Indeed the human race itself is renewed, as the newly baptized throughout the world come to rise in newness of life.

Chromatius of Aquileia
Fourth century

I have more on my mind to express;
I am full like the full moon.
Listen to me, my faithful children, and blossom
    like a rose growing by a stream of water.
Send out fragrance like incense,
    and put forth blossoms like a lily.
Scatter the fragrance, and sing a hymn of praise.   Sirach 39:12–14

THE Jews divide the year into lunar months (sometimes twelve, sometimes thirteen), each of them beginning with the new moon. The Pasch begins on the evening of the 14th of the spring month Nisan, and thus at the full moon. The church, however, did not adhere to the precise date of the fourteenth for her celebration of Easter, although in the second century a party in Asia Minor (the Quartodecimans) strove for this principle. Instead, after a long dispute had raged about this question, Pope Victor (198) decided that Easter should be celebrated everywhere on the Sunday which followed the spring full moon, according to the custom which was by then already predominating.   Josef Jungmann

THE beginning of the Passover is half-way through the month, the fourteenth day, when the moon is at its full, to show that there is no darkness on this day, but that it is full of light, the sun shining from the dawn to the evening, and the moon from the evening to the dawn.   Philo of Alexandria
First century

SING aloud to God our strength;
shout for joy to the God of Jacob.
Raise a song, sound the tambourine,
    the sweet lyre with the harp.
Blow the trumpet
    at the full moon, on our festal day.   Psalm 81:1–3

THE luminous life now triumphs, having scattered the darkness of idolatry in the abundance of its light. This is why the course of the moon, on the fourteenth day, shows it as facing the rays of the sun. Having welcomed the sun when he is setting, she herself does not set before she has mingled her own rays with those of the sun, so that only one light endures without any lack of continuity, through the whole cycle of day and night, with no interval of darkness. Let your whole life, then, be one sole feast and one great day.

Gregory of Nyssa
Fourth century

CAN there be any day but this,
Though many suns to shine endeavor?
We count three hundred, but we miss:
There is but one, and that one ever.

George Herbert
Seventeenth century

IT is the proper function of the liturgy to "make" the church preparation and to reveal her as fulfillment. Every day, every week, every year it is thus transformed and made into this double reality, into a correlation between the "already" and the "not yet." We could not have prepared ourselves for the Kingdom of God which is "yet to come" if the Kingdom were not "already" given to us. We could never have made the *end* an object of love, hope and desire if it were not revealed to us as a glorious and radiant *beginning.* We could never have prayed "Thy Kingdom come!" if we did not have the taste of that Kingdom already communicated to us. If the liturgy of the church would not have been "fulfillment," our life could never have become "preparation." Thus this double rhythm of preparation and fulfillment, far from being accidental, constitutes the very essence of the liturgical life of the church, of the liturgy not only in its totality but also in each of its component parts—each season, each service, each sacrament. What would Pascha be without the white quiet of the Holy and Blessed Sabbath? The solemn darkness of Good Friday without the long lenten preparation? Yet, is not the sadness of Lent made into a "bright sadness" by the light which comes to it from the Pascha it prepares?

Alexander Schmemann

H AVING completed the forty days that bring profit to our souls, we beseech thee in thy love for us: Grant us also to behold thy passion.

Byzantine Vespers

Endnotes

An Order for Daily Prayer

You live in: Psalm 91 from *The Psalms: A New Translation for Prayer and Worship,* translated by Gary Chamberlain. Copyright © 1984, The Upper Room, Nashville, Tennessee. All rights reserved. Used with permission.

Gospel Canticle translations by Gail Ramshaw and Gordon Lathrop.

Third Week of Lent

Tuesday

Kyrie, O God: Translated by W. Gustave Polack. Music can be found in *Lutheran Worship,* #209.

All right: From *Fences,* August Wilson. Published by New American Library, New York.

Thus it was: From *Early Christian Prayers,* edited by A. Hamman, OFM, translated by Walter Mitchell. English translation copyright © 1961, Longmans, Green and Company, Ltd. Published by Henry Regnery Company, Chicago. Used with permission.

Let the mouth: From *The Lenten Spring,* Thomas Hopko. Copyright © 1983, St. Vladimir's Seminary Press. All rights reserved. Used with permission.

Real leadership: From *Assembly,* vol. 8, no. 3. Published by University of Notre Dame Press, Notre Dame, Indiana.

You may not: From *Works,* vol. 1. Published by St. Anthony Guild, 1960.

Thus the: Music can be found in *The Southern Harmony and Musical Companion,* p. 259.

Wednesday

We do not know: "Death and Cosmic Resurrection," from *The Mystery of Suffering and Death,* Michael J. Taylor. Published by Alba House, New York, 1973.

The liturgy: From *The Divine Pity,* Gerald Vann, OP. Published by Image Books, a division of Bantam Doubleday Dell Publishing Group, Inc., New York, 1961.

One may: From *Orthodoxy,* Gilbert K. Chesterton. Published by Image Books, a division of Bantam Doubleday Dell Publishing Group, Inc., New York.

We have: From "We Are All Witnesses: An Interview with Elie Wiesel," in *Parabola,* "Myth and the Quest for Meaning," vol. 10, no. 2. Published by Parabola, New York, 1985.

My dear: From *The Brothers Karamazov,* Fyodor Dostoyevsky, translated by David Magarshack. Published by Penguin Books, Inc., Baltimore, Maryland.

What must: From *Great Lent,* Alexander Schmemann. Copyright © 1969, St. Vladimir's Seminary Press. Used with permission.

I sometimes: From *Telephone Poles and Other Poems,* John Updike. Copyright © 1963, John Updike. Reprinted by permission of Alfred A. Knopf, Inc.

Babies and: From *On Pilgrimage,* Dorothy Day. Published by Catholic Worker Books, New York, 1948.

Like a little drop: From *Asking the Fathers,* Aelred Squire. Published by Morehouse-Barlow, 1973.

When from: Music can be found in the *Lutheran Book of Worship,* #302.

How beautiful: From *The Gift to Be Simple: Songs, Dances and Rituals of the American Shakers,* Edward D. Andrews. Published by Dover Publications, Inc., New York.

Thursday

Dear Lord: From *The Rural Life Prayerbook,* written and compiled by Alban J. Cachauer, SJ. Copyright © 1956, National Catholic Rural Life Conference, Des Moines, Iowa. Used with permission.

O healing: Music can be found in *Gather,* #242.

A spendthrift: Thomas H. Troeger, from *Worship,* #597. Copyright © GIA Publications, Inc., Chicago, Illinois. All rights reserved.

Enter into: From *A City Not Forsaken: Jerusalem Community Rule of Life.* Translation copyright © 1985, Darton, Longman and Todd, Ltd., London.

Men of few words: From *Henry V,* 3.2.

Silence goes: From *The Art of Eating in France: Manners and Menus in the Nineteenth Century,* Jean-Paul Aron. Published by Peter Owen, Ltd., United Kingdom, 1974.

Every year: From *The Way to God, According to the Rule of St. Benedict,* Emmanuel Heufelder, OSB, translated by Luke Eberle, OSB. Copyright © 1983, Cistercian Publications. Reprinted by permission of Cistercian Publications, Inc., Kalamazoo, Michigan; Spencer, Massachusetts.

You know: From *A City Not Forsaken: Jerusalem Community Rule of Life.* Translation copyright © 1985, Darton, Longman and Todd, Ltd., London.

I am as rich: From *The Book of Angelus Silesius,* translated, drawn and handwritten by Frederick Franck. Copyright © 1976, Frederick Franck. Reprinted by permission of Alfred A. Knopf, Inc.

Jerusalem: From *The Psalms: A New Translation for Prayer and Worship,* translated by Gary Chamberlain. Copyright © 1984, The Upper Room, Nashville, Tennessee. All rights reserved. Used with permission.

This is: From *Walden,* Henry David Thoreau. Copyright © 1966, W. W. Norton and Company, Inc., New York.

Lenten ys come: From *The Oxford Book of English Verse,* chosen and edited by Sir Arthur Quiller-Couch. Published by Oxford University Press, New York and Toronto, 1940.

We must: Excerpts from *Seasons of Celebration,* Thomas Merton. Copyright © 1950, 1958, 1962, 1964, 1965, Abbey of Gethsemani. Reprinted by permission of Farrar, Straus and Giroux, Inc.

An altered: From *Great American Poets,* edited by Geoffrey Moore. Published by Clarkson N. Potter, Inc., New York.

Friday

May the One: Excerpts from *A Passover Haggadah* are copyright © 1974, Central Conference of American Rabbis. Used with permission.

All that: From *The Collected Works of St. Teresa of Avila,* vol. 2. Published by the Institute of Carmelite Studies, 1980.

In the last: From *Markings,* Dag Hammarskjöld, translated by Leif Sjoberg and W. H. Auden. Translation copyright © 1964, Alfred A. Knopf, Inc., and Faber and Faber, Ltd. Reprinted by permission of the publisher.

Being bound: Excerpt from *God in Search of Man* by Abraham Joshua Heschel. Copyright © 1955, Abraham Joshua Heschel. Renewal copyright © 1983, Sylvia Heschel. Reprinted by permission of Farrar, Straus and Giroux, Inc.

To love: From *Letters to a Young Poet,* Rainer Maria Rilke, translated by M. D. Herter Norton. Copyright 1934, W. W. Norton and Company; copyright renewed © 1962, M. D. Herter Norton. Revised edition copyright © 1954, W. W. Norton and Company, Inc.; copyright renewed © 1982, M. D. Herter Norton. Used with permission.

Yes—death: From *A Raisin in the Sun.* Copyright © 1959, 1960, Robert Nemiroff as Executor of the Estate of Lorraine Hansberry. Published by The New American Library, New York, 1966.

Awake: F. Bland Tucker, text copyright © 1980, Augsburg Publishing House. Reprinted by permission of Augsburg Fortress. Music can be found in *Worship, #586.*

Every lapse: From *Christ Our Light: Patristic Readings on Gospel Themes,* vol. 1, translated and edited by Friends of Henry Ashworth. Published by Exordium Books, Riverdale, Maryland, 1981.

Fragments of: "Meditation," Gordon Lathrop, from *Paschal Mission 1983,* published by Liturgy Training Publications, Chicago.

You can't: From *Brighton Rock,* Graham Greene. Published by The Viking Press, New York, 1938.

Saturday

Ad te: Music can be found in *The Pius X Hymnal, #202.* Published by McLaughlin and Reilly Company, Boston, 1956.

It was a-thundering: From *Gifts of Power: The Writings of Rebecca Jackson, Black Visionary, Shaker Eldress,* edited by Jean McMahon Humez. Copyright © 1981, The University of Massachusetts Press. Used with permission.

One day: Music can be found in *Songs of Zion, #157.*

Mercy is: From *A Word in Season: Monastic Lectionary for the Divine Office.* Reprinted with permission of Augustinian Press, Villanova, Pennsylvania.

The quality: From *The Merchant of Venice,* 4.1.

Let us pray: From *Early Christian Prayers,* edited by A. Hamman, OFM, translated by Walter Mitchell. English translation copyright © 1961, Longmans, Green and Company, Ltd. Published by Henry Regnery Company, Chicago. Used with permission.

Jesus, Master: Music can be found in *The Summit Choir Book, #71.*

Thus I create: "To Kiss God's Rod," from *Ben Jonson and the Cavalier Poets,* edited by Hugh MacLean. Published by W. W. Norton and Company, New York.

Live a humble: Music can be found in *Songs of Zion, #108.*

There is: Reprinted with permission of Charles Scribner's Sons, an imprint of Macmillan Publishing Company from *The New Being* by Paul Tillich. Copyright © 1955, Paul Tillich; copyright renewed © 1983, Hannah Tillich.

Again the: From *The Blood of the Lamb,* Peter DeVries. Distributed by Warner Books, Inc., a subsidiary of Warner Publishing, Inc., New York.

Fourth Week of Lent

Sunday

There are two: From *The Liturgical Year,* Prosper Guéranger, OSB, translated from the French by Laurence Shepherd, OSB. Reprinted by permission of Paulist Press, Mahwah, New Jersey.

Twenty-five hundred: From *Letters for God's Name,* Gail Ramshaw. Text copyright © 1984, Gail Ramshaw-Schmidt. Reprinted by permission of the author.

As long as: From *A Treasury of Jewish Quotations,* edited by Joseph L. Baron. Copyright © 1956, Joseph L. Baron; copyright © 1965, A. S. Barnes and Co., Inc., South Brunswick, New Jersey.

We are sojourners: From *The Liturgical Year,* Prosper Guéranger, OSB, translated from the French by Laurence Shepherd, OSB. Reprinted by permission of Paulist Press, Mahwah, New Jersey.

We are the pilgrims: From *To Be a Pilgrim,* Joyce Cary. Published by Harper and Row Publishers, Inc., New York, 1942.

It was inch: Music can be found in *Songs of Zion,* #93.

To improvise: "Improvisation," Jared Carter, from *Poetry.* Copyright © 1987, Modern Poetry Association. Reprinted by permission of the editor and the author.

Guide me: Music can be found in *The Hymnal 1982,* #690.

There is no doubt: From *The Divine Pity,* Gerald Vann, OP. Published by Image Books, a division of Bantam Doubleday Dell Publishing Group, Inc., New York, 1961.

City of God: Words by Christopher Idle. Words copyright © 1982, Hope Publishing Company, Carol Stream, Illinois. All rights reserved. Used with permission.

It is the day: Text by George Leonard. From *The Oxford Book of Carols,* reprinted by permission of Oxford University Press.

A Christian: From *The Liturgy of the Church,* Virgil Michel, OSB. Copyright © 1937, The Macmillan Company, New York.

Bright sadness: From *Great Lent,* Alexander Schmemann. Copyright © 1969, St. Vladimir's Seminary Press. Used with permission.

Rejoice: Music can be found in *Lutheran Worship,* #455.

Why should we: From *Sermons on the Liturgy for Sundays and Feast Days,* Pius Parsch, translated by Philip T. Weller. Copyright © 1953, The Bruce Publishing Company, Milwaukee.

The freight: From *Hunting the Divine Fox: Images and Mystery in Christian Faith,* Robert Farrar Capon. Published by The Seabury Press, New York, 1974.

Monday

Oh, Joseph: Music can be found in *The Oxford Book of Carols,* #115.

The words: From *The Reed of God,* Caryll Houselander. Published by Arena Lettres, Waldwick, New Jersey, 1978.

How beautiful: Excerpts from *The Violence of Love* by Oscar Romero, compiled and translated by James R. Brockman. Copyright © 1988, Chicago Province of the Society of Jesus. Reprinted by permission of Harper-Collins Publishers.

From the: From *The Lenten Triodion,* translated by Mother Mary and Archimandrite Kallistos Ware. Reprinted by permission of Faber and Faber, Ltd., London.

This is why: Excerpts from *The Violence of Love* by Oscar Romero, compiled and translated by James R. Brockman. Copyright © 1988, Chicago Province of the Society of Jesus. Reprinted by permission of Harper-Collins Publishers.

The brothers: Reprinted from *Kontakia of Romanos: Byzantine Melodist II: On Christian Life,* translated by Marjorie Carpenter, by permission of the University of Missouri Press. Copyright © 1973, Curators of the University of Missouri.

Let us now: From *The Lenten Triodion,* translated by Mother Mary and Archimandrite Kallistos Ware. Reprinted by permission of Faber and Faber, Ltd., London.

a man: "a man who had fallen among thieves" is reprinted from *IS 5* poems by E. E. Cummings, edited by George James Firmage, by permission of Liveright Publishing Corporation. Copyright © 1985, E. E. Cummings Trust. Copyright © 1926, Horace Liveright. Copyright © 1954, E. E. Cummings. Copyright © 1985, George James Firmage.

I saw: From *The Oxford Book of Prayer,* edited by George Appleton. Published in the United States by Oxford University Press, New York.

Christ: "The Face of Christ," from *The World for Wedding Ring,* Daniel J. Berrigan, SJ. Published by Macmillan Publishing Company, New York.

Jerusalem's: From *The Psalms: A New Translation for Prayer and Worship,* translated by Gary Chamberlain. Copyright © 1984, The Upper Room, Nashville, Tennessee. All rights reserved. Used with permission.

Then follows: From *The Lenten Triodion,* translated by Mother Mary and Archimandrite Kallistos Ware. Reprinted by permission of Faber and Faber, Ltd., London.

Genuine forgiveness: Reprinted with permission of Charles Scribner's Sons, an imprint of Macmillan Publishing Company from *The New Being* by Paul Tillich. Copyright © 1955, Paul Tillich; copyright renewed © 1983, Hannah Tillich.

Tuesday

A cup: From *The Gift to Be Simple: Songs, Dances and Rituals of the American Shakers,* Edward D. Andrews. Published by Dover Publications, Inc., New York.

God our mother: From *Resources for Ritual.* Copyright © 1987, Medical Mission Sisters, Philadelphia, Pennsylvania. Published by Meyer Stone Books, Oak Park, Illinois.

The only reason: From *Christ Our Light: Patristic Readings on Gospel Themes,* vol. 1, translated and edited by Friends of Henry Ashworth. Published by Exordium Books, Riverdale, Maryland, 1981.

in Just-: Reprinted from *Tulips & Chimneys* by E. E. Cummings, edited by George James Firmage, by permission of Liveright Publishing Corporation. Copyright 1923, 1925; renewed 1951, 1953, E. E. Cummings. Copyright © 1973, 1976. Trustees for the E. E. Cummings Trust. Copyright © 1973, 1976, George James Firmage.

The jasmine: From *An Interrupted Life: The Diaries of Etty Hillesum, 1941–1943,* Etty Hillesum, translated by Arno Pomerans. Translation copyright © 1983, Jonathan Cape, Ltd. Reprinted by permission of Pantheon Books, a division of Random House, Inc.

I want: Kathleen Thomerson. Copyright © 1970, 1975, Celebration. Admin. by Maranatha! Music, Laguna Hills, California. Music can be found in *Gather,* #208.

Give us: Excerpts from *God under My Roof* by Esther de Waal. Copyright © 1984, Sisters of the Love of God. Available from Paraclete Press, Orleans, Massachusetts. Used with permission.

Fasting is: From *The Lenten Spring,* Thomas Hopko. Copyright © 1983, St. Vladimir's Seminary Press. All rights reserved. Used with permission.

Our only: Excerpts from "East Coker" and "Little Gidding" in *The Four Quartets.* Copyright © 1943, T. S. Eliot; copyright renewed © 1971, Esme Valerie Eliot, reprinted by permission of Harcourt Brace Jovanovich, Inc.

So that's: From *The Blood of the Lamb,* Peter DeVries. Distributed by Warner Books, Inc., a susbidiary of Warner Publishing, Inc., New York.

Wednesday

We got used to: Excerpts from *A Passover Haggadah* are copyright © 1974, Central Conference of American Rabbis. Used with permission.

With Amen: From Symphony No. 3, "Kaddish," Leonard Bernstein. Copyright © 1963, Leonard Bernstein.

many books: "Pan Cogito Seeks Counsel," Zbigniew Herbert, translated by James P. Barron, OP, from *Męczeństwo i zagłada Żydow w zapisach literatury polskiej,* edited and collected by Irena Maciejewska. Copyright © 1988, Krajowa Agencja Wydawnia, Warsaw.

O Lord: From the *New American Bible with Revised New Testament.* Copyright © 1986, Confraternity of Christian Doctrine, used by license of the copyright owner. All rights reserved. No part of the *New American Bible with Revised New Testament* may be reproduced in any form without permission in writing from the copyright owner.

Thou hast: From *The Lenten Triodion,* translated by Mother Mary and Archimandrite Kallistos Ware. Reprinted by permission of Faber and Faber, Ltd., London.

A mother: From *Revelations of Divine Love,* Julian of Norwich. Copyright © 1966, Clifton Wolters. Published by Viking Penguin, Inc., New York.

Mary modyr: Anonymous, in *The Oxford Book of Christian Verse,* edited by Lord David Cecil. Published by Oxford University Press, London.

Christianity: From *The Origins of the Liturgical Year,* Thomas J. Talley. Published by Pueblo Publishing Company, New York, 1986. Used with permission.

The threefold: "The Mother of God," William Butler Yeats. Reprinted with permission of Macmillan Publishing Company from *The Poems of W. B. Yeats: A New Edition,* edited by Richard J. Finneran. Copyright © 1933, Macmillan Publishing Company; copyright renewed © 1961, Bertha Georgie Yeats.

Gabriel's message: Music can be found in *The Hymnal 1982,* #270.

Let in: "Northumbrian Sequence IV," *Collected Poems of Kathleen Raine.* Copyright © 1965, Kathleen Raine. Reprinted by permission of Hamish Hamilton, Ltd., London.

The eternal: From *Mary, Mother of the Lord,* Karl Rahner. Reprinted with permission of Herder and Herder, The Crossroad/Continuum Publishing Company, New York.

Thursday

To praise: Excerpt from *The Quino Elegies and Sonnets to Orpheus,* Rainer Maria Rilke, translated by A. Poulin, Jr. Copyright © 1975, 1976, 1977, A. Poulin, Jr. Reprinted by permission of Houghton Mifflin Company.

The boy stood: Excerpt from *The Violent Bear It Away,* Flannery O'Connor. Copyright © 1964, 1965, Estate of Mary Flannery O'Connor. Reprinted by permission of Farrar, Straus and Giroux, Inc.

I was: From *Early Christian Prayers,* edited by A. Hamman, OFM, translated by Walter Mitchell. English translation copyright © 1961, Longmans, Green and Company, Ltd. Published by Henry Regnery Company, Chicago. Used with permission.

We are: From a speech delivered on April 3, 1968, Memphis, Tennessee, in *Martin Luther King, Jr.: A Documentary . . . Montgomery to Memphis.* Published by W. W. Norton and Company, New York. Copyright © Martin Luther King, Jr. and Estate of Martin Luther King, Jr. Reprinted by permission of Joan Daves.

In an alley: From *Brighton Rock,* Graham Greene. Published by The Viking Press, New York, 1938.

Look at: From *The Psalms: A New Translation for Prayer and Worship,* translated by Gary Chamberlain. Copyright © 1984, The Upper Room, Nashville, Tennessee. All rights reserved. Used with permission.

Fasting: From *Troparia and Kondakia,* translated and published by the Monks of New Skete, Cambridge, New York.

But that: From "Riding Westward" John Donne, in *The Oxford Book of English Mystical Verse.* Published by Oxford University Press, London, 1917.

Through the: From *Signs, Words and Gestures,* Balthasar Fischer, translated by Matthew J. O'Connell. Copyright © 1981, Pueblo Publishing Company, New York. Used with permission.

Nowadays: From *Primitive Christian Symbols,* Jean Daniélou, SJ, translated by Donald Attwater. English translation copyright © 1964. Burns and Oates, Ltd. Used with permission.

We should: From *A Word in Season: Monastic Lectionary for the Divine Office.* Reprinted with permission of Augustinian Press, Villanova, Pennsylvania.

Paul, when: Excerpt from *Best Sermons I,* James W. Cox. Copyright © 1988, Kathryn Spink. Reprinted by permission of HarperCollins Publishers

One day: From *Souls on Fire,* Elie Wiesel. Copyright © 1972, Elie Wiesel. Reprinted with permission of Summit Books, a division of Simon and Schuster, Inc.

Friday

Remember: From *The Macmillan Book of Earliest Christian Hymns,* edited by F. Forrester Church and Terrence J. Multry. Copyright © 1988, F. Forrester Church and Terrence J. Multry. Published by Macmillan Publishing Company, New York.

Our immaturity: From *Troparia and Kondakia,* translated and published by the Monks of New Skete, Cambridge, New York.

When the: Excerpts from "Choruses from the Rock" in *Collected Poems 1909–1962.* Copyright © 1936, Harcourt Brace Jovanovich, Inc.; copyright © 1964, 1963, T. S. Eliot, reprinted by permission of the publisher.

If life: From *A Matter of Eternity, Selections from the Writings of Dorothy L. Sayers.* Published by William B. Eerdmans Publishing Company, Grand Rapids, Michigan.

Cleanse: From the *New American Bible with Revised New Testament.* Copyright © 1986, Confraternity of Christian Doctrine, used by license of the copyright owner. All rights reserved. No part of the *New American Bible with Revised New Testament* may be reproduced in any form without permission in writing from the copyright owner.

I would not: Music can be found in *Songs of Zion,* #99.

Along with: From *The Psalms: A New Translation for Prayer and Worship,* translated by Gary Chamberlain. Copyright © 1984, The Upper Room, Nashville, Tennessee. All rights reserved. Used with permission.

Resh Lakish said: From *A Rabbinic Anthology,* selected and arranged by C. G. Montefiore and H. Loewe. Published by Schocken Books, Inc., New York.

I heard: "The Dream of the Rood," translated by Gail Ramshaw. Copyright © The Liturgical Conference, Washington, D.C. All rights reserved. Used with permission.

Let me: Excerpts from *The Violence of Love* by Oscar Romero, compiled and translated by James R. Brockman. Copyright © 1988, Chicago Province of the Society of Jesus. Reprinted by permission of HarperCollins Publishers.

You can: From *Mass, A Theatre Piece for Singers, Players and Dancers,* Leonard Bernstein.

Behold it: From *The Gift to Be Simple: Songs, Dances and Rituals of the American Shakers,* Edward D. Andrews. Published by Dover Publications, Inc., New York.

The story: From *To Live as We Worship,* Lawrence E. Mick. Published by The Liturgical Press, Collegeville, 1984.

I need: From *Hope and Suffering,* Desmond Tutu. Published by William B. Eerdmans Publishing Company, Grand Rapids, Michigan, 1984.

A lamb: Paul Gerhardt, translated by Henry L. Letterman. Text copyright © 1982, Concordia Publishing House. Reprinted by permission of Concordia Publishing House. Music can be found in *Lutheran Worship,* #111.

God in heaven: From *Morning, Noon and Night,* edited by John Carden. Published by the Church Missionary Society.

Almighty God: From *The Book of Common Prayer,* according to the use of the Episcopal Church. Published by The Seabury Press, New York, 1979.

Saturday

Jesus' words: From *The Two-Edged Sword: An Interpretation of the Old Testament,* John L. McKenzie, SJ. Copyright © 1956, The Bruce Publishing Company, Milwaukee.

It is curious: From *A Matter of Eternity, Selections from the Writings of Dorothy L. Sayers.* Copyright © 1947, Dorothy L. Sayers. Copyright © 1973, William B. Eerdmans Publishing Company, Grand Rapids, Michigan.

The church's: Excerpts from *The Violence of Love* by Oscar Romero, compiled and translated by James R. Brockman. Copyright © 1988, Chicago Province of the Society of Jesus. Reprinted by permission of Harper-Collins Publishers.

The greatness: From *The Library of Christian Classics,* vol. 1. Published by The Westminster Press, 1953.

Atonement means: From *The Predicament of the Prosperous,* Bruce C. Birch and Larry Rasmussen. Published by The Westminster Press, 1978.

Alas! and did: Music can be found in the *Lutheran Book of Worship,* #98.

We can: From "Discipleship and the Cross," *The Cost of Discipleship,* Dietrich Bonhoeffer. Published by Macmillan Publishing Company, New York, 1959.

How easy: Reprinted with permission of Macmillan Publishing Company from *The Diary of a Country Priest,* Georges Bernanos, translated by Pamela Morris. Copyright © 1937, copyright renewed © 1965, Macmillan Publishing Company.

It is certain: From *A Word in Season: Monastic Lectionary for the Divine Office.* Reprinted with permission of Augustinian Press, Villanova, Pennsylvania.

When I survey: Music can be found in *The Hymnal, 1982,* #474.

The whole: From *Sign of Contradiction,* Karol Wojtyła. Published by The Seabury Press, New York, 1979.

The waves: From *The Psalms: A New Translation for Prayer and Worship,* translated by Gary Chamberlain. Copyright © 1984, The Upper Room, Nashville, Tennessee. All rights reserved. Used with permission.

All is in: From "That Nature Is a Heraclitean Fire and of the Comfort of the Resurrection," Gerard Manley Hopkins.

Fifth Week of Lent

Sunday

During Lent: From *Public Worship: A Survey,* Josef A. Jungmann, SJ, translated by Clifford Howell, SJ. Published by The Liturgical Press, Collegeville.

You, neighbor: From *Poems from the Book of Hours,* Rainer Maria Rilke, translated by Babette Deutsch. Copyright © 1946, New Directions Corporation. Reprinted by permission of New Directions Publishing Corporation.

O sun: From "Psalm 139," Mary Herbert, in *The Oxford Book of Christian Verse,* edited by Lord David Cecil. Published by Oxford University Press, London.

I look: From *The Psalms: A New Translation for Prayer and Worship,* translated by Gary Chamberlain. Copyright © 1984, The Upper Room, Nashville, Tennessee. All rights reserved. Used with permission.

Without the: From *The Pain of Christ and the Sorrow of God,* Gerald Vann, OP. Published by Blackfriars, London, 1957.

I have no: From "A Better Resurrection," Christina Georgina Rossetti, in *The Oxford Book of Christian Verse,* edited by Lord David Cecil. Published by Oxford University Press, London.

The same: "In Hardwood Groves" from *The Complete Poems of Robert Frost.* Published by Holt, Rinehart and Winston, Inc., Orlando, Florida, 1962.

Now green: "I Know a Village," *Times Three, Selected Verse from Three Decades,* Phyllis McGinley. Published by Image Books, a division of Bantam Doubleday Dell Publishing Group, Inc., New York, 1975.

The human race: From *Christ Our Light: Patristic Readings on Gospel Themes,* vol. 1, translated and edited by Friends of Henry Ashworth. Published by Exordium Books, Riverdale, Maryland, 1981.

Before the fruit: Text by Thomas H. Troeger. Music can be found in *Worship,* #418.

To each: Excerpts from *The Violence of Love* by Oscar Romero, compiled and translated by James R. Brockman. Copyright © 1988, Chicago Province of the Society of Jesus. Reprinted by permission of HarperCollins Publishers.

Perish the sword: "Let there be light," Frances W. Davis. Text copyright © American Peace Society. Used with permission.

We shall: "From the Dark Tower," Countée Cullen, from the collection of poems *On These I Stand.* Published by Harper and Bros., New York, 1947.

To you: From *The Rural Life Prayerbook,* written and compiled by Alban J. Cachauer, SJ. Copyright © 1956, National Catholic Rural Life Conference, Des Moines, Iowa. Used with permission.

We plough: Music can be found in *The Hymnal 1982,* #264.

Hear, O Father: Excerpts from opening prayers for Mass of the Italian sacramentary, *Messale Romano.* Copyright © 1983, Libreria Editrice Vaticana. Translated by Peter Scagnelli.

Monday

Instead of: From *Great Lent,* Alexander Schmemann. Copyright © 1969, St. Vladimir's Seminary Press. Used with permission.

It is not: "On Suffering," *Letters and Papers from Prison.* Published by SCM Press, 1967.

I knew: From *Herself Surprised,* Joyce Cary. Published by Harper and Row Publishers, Inc., New York, 1941.

Though I: From *Everyman and Medieval Miracle Plays,* edited by A. C. Cawley. Reprinted by permission of J. M. Dent and Sons, Ltd., London.

And now: From *Go Tell It on the Mountain,* James Baldwin. Published by Dial Press, New York, 1963.

Let the sinner: From *Christ Our Light: Patristic Readings on Gospel Themes,* vol. 1, translated and edited by Friends of Henry Ashworth. Published by Exordium Books, Riverdale, Maryland, 1981.

The Christian: Reprinted with permission from *Jesus in Focus: A Life in Its Setting* by Twenty-Third Publications, Mystic, Connecticut. Copyright © 1983, Gerard S. Sloyan.

This thought: From *The Assistant,* Bernard Malamud. Published by Farrar, Straus and Giroux, Inc., New York, 1957.

Too much searching: From *Conjectures of a Guilty Bystander,* Thomas Merton. Published by Bantam Doubleday Dell Publishing Group, Inc., New York, 1966.

Tuesday

As on: From *Wyeth's Repository of Sacred Music, Part Second,* Harrisburg, Pennsylvania, 1820.

Yom Kippur: From *Night,* Elie Wiesel. English translation copyright © 1960, MacGibbon & Kee. Published by Avon Books, a division of The Hearst Corporation, New York.

I would: "Bread," Ila and Henia Karmel, translated by James P. Barron, OP, from *Anthology of Verse about the Jews and the German Occupation,* M. M. Borwicz, from *Męczeństwo i zagłada Żydow w zapisach literatury polskiej,* edited and collected by Irena Maciejewska. Copyright © 1988, Krajowa Agencja Wydawnia, Warsaw.

Affliction: Reprinted by permission of The Putnam Publishing Group from *Waiting for God,* Simone Weil. Copyright © 1951, G. P. Putnam's Sons; renewed 1979.

I am not: From *An Interrupted Life: The Diaries of Etty Hillesum, 1941–1943,* Etty Hillesum, translated by Arno Pomerans. Translation copyright © 1983, Jonathan Cape, Ltd. Reprinted by permission of Pantheon Books, a division of Random House, Inc.

O the beautiful: From *The Gift to Be Simple: Songs, Dances and Rituals of the American Shakers,* Edward D. Andrews. Published by Dover Publications, Inc., New York.

It is: From *New Seeds of Contemplation,* Thomas Merton. Copyright © 1961, Abbey of Gethsemani, Inc. Reprinted by permission of New Directions Publishing Corporation.

The moon: Music can be found in *The Oxford Book of Carols,* #46.

Humility comes: From *Living Prayer,* Anthony Bloom. Published by Templegate Publishers, Springfield, Illinois.

We humbly: From *The Rural Life Prayerbook,* written and compiled by Alban J. Cachauer, SJ. Copyright © 1956, National Catholic Rural Life Conference, Des Moines, Iowa. Used with permission.

Change and: From *In the Kingdom of the Lonely God,* Robert Griffin. Published by Paulist Press, Mahwah, New Jersey. Used with permission.

Christ: Music can be found in *Lutheran Worship,* #94.

I late estrang'd: From *Wyeth's Repository of Sacred Music, Part Second,* Harrisburg, Pennsylvania, 1820.

O you: From *Troparia and Kondakia,* translated and published by the Monks of New Skete, Cambridge, New York.

When the doctor: "The Cast," Sharon Olds, from *Poetry.* Copyright © 1985, Modern Poetry Association. Reprinted by permission of the editor and the author.

Wednesday

When the layers: Reprinted with permission of Atheneum Publishers, an imprint of Macmillan Publishing Company, from *The Last of the Just,* André Schwarz-Bart, translated from the French by Stephen Becker. Copyright © 1960, Atheneum Publishers.

O sages: From "Sailing to Byzantium," William Butler Yeats. Reprinted with permission of Macmillan Publishing Company from *The Poems of W. B. Yeats: A New Edition,* edited by Richard J. Finneran. Copyright © 1928, Macmillan Publishing Company; copyright renewed © 1956, Bertha Georgie Yeats.

Come, my: From *The Oxford Book of Prayer,* edited by George Appleton. Published in the United States by Oxford University Press, New York.

One who: Excerpt from *Why We Can't Wait,* Martin Luther King, Jr. Copyright © 1963, 1964, Martin Luther King, Jr. Reprinted by permission of HarperCollins Publishers.

When Polycarp: From "The Martyrdom of Polycarp," *Ancient Christian Writers,* vol. 6. Published by Paulist Press, Mahwah, New Jersey, 1948. Used with permission.

May my song: From *The Prayers of Man: From Primitive Peoples to Present Times,* compiled by Alfonso M. diNola, edited by Patrick O'Connor. Published by Ivan Obolensky, Inc., New York, 1961. This formula was adopted for the benediction of incense in the Salisbury Church.

The meaning: From *Signs, Words and Gestures,* Balthasar Fischer, translated by Matthew J. O'Connell. Copyright © 1981, Pueblo Publishing Company, New York. Used with permission.

That, then: From *A Word in Season: Monastic Lectionary for the Divine Office.* Reprinted with permission of Augustinian Press, Villanova, Pennsylvania.

Thursday

If God: From *Tossing and Turning,* John Updike. Copyright © 1977, John Updike. Reprinted by permission of Alfred A. Knopf, Inc.

The world said: Excerpt from *The Violent Bear It Away,* Flannery O'Connor. Copyright © 1964, 1965, Estate of Mary Flannery O'Connor. Reprinted by permission of Farrar, Straus and Giroux, Inc.

Love is not: From *Flannery O'Connor and the Mystery of Love,* Richard Giannone. Published by the University of Illinois Press, Urbana and Chicago, 1989.

When the fast: From *The Lenten Spring,* Thomas Hopko. Copyright © 1983, St. Vladimir's Seminary Press. All rights reserved. Used with permission.

Those struck: Reprinted by permission of The Putnam Publishing Group from *Waiting for God,* Simone Weil. Copyright © 1951, G. P. Putnam's Sons; renewed 1979.

O mortal one: Music can be found in *The Oxford Book of Carols,* #45.

The people: From *A Matter of Eternity, Selections from the Writings of Dorothy L. Sayers.* Copyright © 1947, Dorothy L. Sayers. Copyright © 1973, William B. Eerdmans Publishing Company, Grand Rapids, Michigan.

He is: Music can be found in *The Summit Choir Book,* #481.

There are: From "Way of the Cross, Way of Justice," Leonardo Boff.

When all: From *An Offering of Uncles: The Priesthood of Adam and the Shape of the World,* Robert Farrar Capon. Published by Harper and Row Publishers, Inc., New York, 1967.

I say: From *From the Fathers to the Churches,* edited by Brother Kenneth, CGA. Compilation copyright © 1983, William Collins Sons and Company, Ltd. Published by Collins Liturgical Publications, London.

The Rabbis: From *The Jewish Way,* Rabbi Irving Greenberg. Copyright © 1988, Irving Greenberg. Reprinted by permission of Summit Books, a division of Simon and Schuster, Inc.

The third: From *From the Fathers to the Churches,* edited by Brother Kenneth, CGA. Compilation copyright © 1983, William Collins Sons and Company, Ltd. Published by Collins Liturgical Publications, London.

And the Son: Excerpts from "Choruses from the Rock" in *Collected Poems 1909–1962.* Copyright © 1936, Harcourt Brace Jovanovich, Inc.; copyright © 1964, 1963, T. S. Eliot, reprinted by permission of the publisher.

Almighty God: From *The Book of Common Prayer,* according to the use of the Episcopal Church. Published by The Seabury Press, New York, 1979.

Friday

O tough: From *A Word in Season: Monastic Lectionary for the Divine Office.* Reprinted with permission of Augustinian Press, Villanova, Pennsylvania.

The crucifixion: Reprinted from *The Prophetic Imagination,* Walter Brueggemann. Copyright © 1978, Fortress Press. Used by permission of Augsburg Fortress.

Look, my soul: Translated by James P. Barron, OP.

This mutilated: "Horae Canonicae," from *W. H. Auden: Collected Poems,* edited by Edward Mendelson. Copyright © 1976, Edward Mendelson, William Meredith and Monroe K. Spears. Reprinted by permission of Random House, Inc.

The paper: From *Burger's Daughter,* Nadine Gordimer. Published by The Viking Press, New York, 1979.

Going to: From *The Lenten Triodion,* translated by Mother Mary and Archimandrite Kallistos Ware. Reprinted by permission of Faber and Faber, Ltd., London.

We have to: From *A Word in Season: Monastic Lectionary for the Divine Office.* Reprinted by permission of Augustinian Press, Villanova, Pennsylvania.

Those who: From *A Word in Season: Monastic Lectionary for the Divine Office.* Reprinted by permission of Augustinian Press, Villanova, Pennsylvania.

The sight: From *Christ Our Light: Readings on Gospel Themes,* vol. 2, translated and edited by Friends of Henry Ashworth. Published by Exordium Books, Riverdale, Maryland, 1985.

This is the day: Music can be found in *Songs of Zion,* #42.

Saturday

We too: From *Christ Our Light: Readings on Gospel Themes,* vol. 2, translated and edited by Friends of Henry Ashworth. Published by Exordium Books, Riverdale, Maryland, 1985.

Even the dead: From *The Psalms: A New Translation for Prayer and Worship,* translated by Gary Chamberlain. Copyright © 1984, The Upper Room, Nashville, Tennessee. All rights reserved. Used with permission.

When Jesus: Music can be found in *The Hymnal 1982,* #715.

There is: Reprinted from *The Prophetic Imagination,* Walter Brueggemann. Copyright © 1978, Fortress Press. Used by permission of Augsburg Fortress.

Eternal Father: Excerpts from opening prayers for Mass of the Italian sacramentary, *Messale Romano.* Copyright © 1983, Libreria Editrice Vaticana. Translated by Peter Scagnelli.

O Christ: From *The Lenten Triodion,* translated by Mother Mary and Archimandrite Kallistos Ware. Reprinted by permission of Faber and Faber, Ltd., London.

We are told how: From *To Dance with God: Family Ritual and Community Celebration,* Gertrud Mueller Nelson, with illustrations by the author. Copyright © 1986, Gertrud Mueller Nelson. Reprinted by permission of the author and Paulist Press, Mahwah, New Jersey.

We are told that: From *Christ Our Light: Patristic Readings on Gospel Themes,* vol. 1, translated and edited by Friends of Henry Ashworth. Published by Exordium Books, Riverdale, Maryland, 1981.

There are often: From *The Fourth Gospel,* Louis Bouyer, translated by Patrick Byrne, SM, STL. English translation copyright © 1964, Newman Press. Reprinted by permission of Paulist Press, Mahwah, New Jersey.

We do not: From *A Martyr's Message of Hope, Six Homilies* by Archbishop Oscar Romero. Published by Celebration Books, Kansas City, Missouri, 1981.

Sixth Week of Lent

Palm Sunday

Whan that Aprill: From *The Canterbury Tales,* Geoffrey Chaucer, edited by A. C. Cawley. Reprinted by permission of Everyman's Library, E. P. Dutton, New York.

April prepares: From *John Mistletoe,* Christopher Morley. Published by Bantam Doubleday Dell Publishing Group, Inc., Garden City, New York.

As the eleventh: From "Diary of a Pilgrimage," *Ancient Christian Writers,* vol. 38. Published by Paulist Press, Mahwah, New Jersey, 1970. Used with permission.

In the tenth century: From *Public Worship: A Survey,* Josef A. Jungmann, SJ, translated by Clifford Howell, SJ. Published by The Liturgical Press, Collegeville.

Bishop Theodulph: From *Early Christian Hymns,* Daniel Joseph Donahoe. Published by The Grafton Press, New York, 1908.

Gloria: Music can be found in *The Pius X Hymnal,* p. 318. Published by McLaughlin & Reilly Company, Boston, 1956.

A city: From *The Jewish Way,* Rabbi Irving Greenberg. Copyright © 1988, Irving Greenberg. Reprinted by permission of Summit Books, a division of Simon and Schuster, Inc.

King Jesus: "Ride on, Jesus, ride," from *Lead Me, Guide Me,* #264. Copyright © GIA Publications, Inc., Chicago, Illinois. All rights reserved.

Fair and: From *Hymns of the Resurrection,* from *Harp of the Spirit,* edited and translated by Sebastian Grock. Published by the Fellowship of St. Alban and St. Sergius, London.

We were: From *The Blood of the Lamb,* Peter DeVries. Distributed by Warner Books, Inc., a subsidiary of Warner Publishing, Inc., New York.

It is ourselves: From *From the Fathers to the Churches,* edited by Brother Kenneth, CGA. Compilation copyright © 1983, William Collins Sons and Company, Ltd. Published by Collins Liturgical Publications, London.

For the church: Excerpts from *The Violence of Love* by Oscar Romero, compiled and translated by James R. Brockman. Copyright © 1988, Chicago Province of the Society of Jesus. Reprinted by permission of Harper-Collins Publishers.

One who has: From *Markings,* Dag Hammarskjöld, translated by Leif Sjoberg and W. H. Auden. Translation copyright © 1964, Alfred A. Knopf, Inc., and Faber and Faber, Ltd. Reprinted by permission of the publisher.

Monday

Said Judas: "Said Judas to Mary," Sydney Carter, from *Worship,* #644. Copyright © GIA Publications, Inc., Chicago, Illinois. All rights reserved.

It is no: From *Signs, Words and Gestures,* Balthasar Fischer, translated by Matthew J. O'Connell. Copyright © 1981, Pueblo Publishing Company, New York. Used with permission.

His voice: Music can be found in *The Southern Harmony and Musical Companion,* p. 322.

O Redeemer: From the English-Latin Roman Missal for the United States of America. Copyright © 1964, United States Catholic Conference (Formerly National Catholic Welfare Conference).

Think, wretched soul: From *The Lenten Triodion,* translated by Mother Mary and Archimandrite Kallistos Ware. Reprinted by permission of Faber and Faber, Ltd., London.

When the church: From *Christ Our Light: Readings on Gospel Themes,* vol. 2, translated and edited by Friends of Henry Ashworth. Published by Exordium Books, Riverdale, Maryland, 1985.

Let those: Reprinted from *Kontakia of Romanos: Byzantin.. Melodist II: On Christian Life,* translated by Marjorie Carpenter, by permission of the University of Missouri Press. Copyright © 1973, Curators of the University of Missouri.

Lord our God: Excerpts from opening prayers for Mass of the Italian sacramentary, *Messale Romano.* Copyright © 1983, Libreria Editrice Vaticana. Translated by Peter Scagnelli.

I have: From *The Gift to Be Simple: Songs, Dances and Rituals of the American Shakers,* Edward D. Andrews. Published by Dover Publications, Inc., New York.

Spring is: From *Mrs. Beeton's Book of Household Management,* Isabella Mary Mayson Beeton. Published by London, Ward, Lock and Tyler, Ltd., 1861.

Monday through: From *To Dance with God: Family Ritual and Community Celebration,* Gertrud Mueller Nelson, with illustrations by the author. Copyright © 1986, Gertrud Mueller Nelson. Reprinted by permission of the author and Paulist Press, Mahwah, New Jersey.

Originally the: From *The New Westminster Dictionary of Liturgy and Worship,* edited by J. G. Davies. Copyright © 1986, SCM Press. Published by The Westminster Press, Philadelphia.

According to: From *Liturgies of the Religious Orders,* Archdale A. King. Published by Longmans, Green and Company, Ltd., London, 1955.

Chametz: From *The Jewish Way,* Rabbi Irving Greenberg. Copyright © 1988, Irving Greenberg. Reprinted by permission of Summit Books, a division of Simon and Schuster, Inc.

So intense: From *The Jewish Party Book,* Mae Shafter Rockland. Published by Schocken Books, Inc., New York.

They were: From *The Earth Is the Lord's and The Sabbath,* Abraham Joshua Heschel. *The Earth Is the Lord's* copyright © 1950, Henry Schuman, Inc. *The Sabbath* copyright © 1951, 1952, Abraham Joshua Heschel. Published by Harper and Row Publishers, Inc., New York.

Tuesday

Perhaps God: From *Orthodoxy,* Gilbert K. Chesterton. Published by Image Books, a division of Bantam Doubleday Dell Publishing Group, Inc., New York.

Not only: Excerpts from *A Passover Haggadah* are copyright © 1974, Central Conference of American Rabbis. Used with permission.

Had God brought: Excerpts from *A Passover Haggadah* are copyright © 1974, Central Conference of American Rabbis. Used with permission.

I am content: Translated by August Crull, 1845–1923. Music can be found in *Lutheran Worship*, #145.

In judging: From "Way of the Cross, Way of Justice," Leonardo Boff.

Above all else: From *Freedom Is Coming: Songs of Protest and Praise,* Anders Nyberg. Published by Utryk, Uppsala, 1984.

Pity me: "Lament of Our Lady at the Foot of the Cross," translated by David Welsh, from *Monumenta Polonica: The First Four Centuries of Polish Poetry,* Bogdana Carpenter. Reprinted with permission of Bogdana Carpenter.

At the Cross: Ascribed to Jocapone da Todi, 1306. Translated by Edward Caswall, 1878. Music can be found in *The Pius X Hymnal,* #201. Published by McLaughlin & Reilly Company, Boston, 1956.

I lie: Excerpts from *God under My Roof* by Esther de Waal. Copyright © 1984, Sisters of the Love of God. Available from Paraclete Press, Orleans, Massachusetts. Used with permission.

Wednesday

Once Mary: Music can be found in *The Oxford Book of Carols,* #93.

It was on: Music can be found in *The Oxford Book of Carols,* #17.

O gracious: Henry Constable, in *The Oxford Book of Christian Verse,* edited by Lord David Cecil. Published by Oxford University Press, London.

The prisoners: From *Aunt Dan and Lemon,* Wallace Shawn. Copyright © 1985, Wallace Shawn. Used by permission of Grove Press, Inc., New York.

No one: From "The Life of St. Francis," *The Classics of Western Spirituality.* Published by Paulist Press, Mahwah, New Jersey, 1978. Used with permission.

He, who navigated: "Death of a Young Son by Drowning," Margaret Atwood, in *The Norton Introduction to Literature.* Published by W. W. Norton and Company, New York.

Death, like: From *Wyeth's Repository of Sacred Music, Part Second,* Harrisburg, Pennsylvania, 1820.

One only: From "The Crucifixion," Alice Meynell, in *The Oxford Book of Christian Verse,* edited by Lord David Cecil. Published by Oxford University Press, London.

When Tim's: From *Nuns and Soldiers,* Iris Murdoch. Copyright © 1980, Iris Murdoch. Reprinted by permission of Viking Penguin, a division of Penguin Books USA, Inc.

Just as: From *The Inferno,* Dante Alighieri, translated by John Ciardi. Published by New American Library, New York.

I have: From the poem "Ocean," Juan Ramón Jiménez, translated by Robert Bly.

Holy Thursday

I tol' Jesus: Music can be found in *Songs of Zion,* #118.

That is: Excerpts from *The Violence of Love* by Oscar Romero, compiled and translated by James R. Brockman. Copyright © 1988, Chicago Province of the Society of Jesus. Reprinted by permission of HarperCollins Publishers.

We must: From *Christ Our Light: Patristic Readings on Gospel Themes,* vol. 1, translated and edited by Friends of Henry Ashworth. Published by Exordium Books, Riverdale, Maryland, 1981.

Maundy Thursday: From *Public Worship: A Survey,* Josef A. Jungmann, SJ, translated by Clifford Howell, SJ. Published by The Liturgical Press, Collegeville.

Jesus, I: From *Early Christian Prayers,* edited by A. Hamman, OFM, translated by Walter Mitchell. English translation copyright © 1961, Longmans, Green and Company, Ltd. Published by Henry Regnery Company, Chicago. Used with permission.

Not by annihilating: From *The Two-Edged Sword: An Interpretation of the Old Testament,* John L. McKenzie, SJ. Copyright © 1956, The Bruce Publishing Company, Milwaukee.

The firstfruits: From *The Lenten Triodion,* translated by Mother Mary and Archimandrite Kallistos Ware. Reprinted by permission of Faber and Faber, Ltd., London.

The Jews: From *Public Worship: A Survey,* Josef A. Jungmann, SJ, translated by Clifford Howell, SJ. Published by The Liturgical Press, Collegeville.

The beginning: From *The Bible and the Liturgy,* Jean Daniélou, SJ. Published by University of Notre Dame Press, Notre Dame, Indiana, 1956.

The luminous: From *The Bible and the Liturgy,* Jean Daniélou, SJ. Published by University of Notre Dame Press, Notre Dame, Indiana, 1956.

Can there: "I Got Me Flowers to Strew Thy Way," George Herbert, in *The New Oxford Book of English Verse,* chosen and edited by Helen Gardner. Published by Oxford University Press, London and New York, 1972.

It is: From *Of Water and the Spirit: A Liturgical Study of Baptism,* Alexander Schmemann. Copyright © 1974, St. Vladimir's Seminary Press. Used with permission.

Having completed: From *The Lenten Triodion,* translated by Mother Mary and Archimandrite Kallistos Ware. Reprinted by permission of Faber and Faber, Ltd., London.